Folie à deux

"Until prison do us part"

Nico Claux

©**Serial Pleasures**, 2024

www.serialpleasures.com

ISBN: 979-8-33528-815-6

Table of contents

The two-headed freak show

According to psychiatrists, "folie a deux" is a rare disorder characterized by the sharing of a specific delusion between two or more people in a relationship. The inducer, who is prey to a delusional psychotic disorder, influences another individual or more, based on his or her delusional beliefs. This disorder is commonly seen in two individuals, but in rare cases it may include larger groups.

As you can see, this term is quite all-encompassing, and can be used to characterize the dynamics of a cult, for example. But it is in the framework of criminology that I chose to explore this term, more particularly to describe relationships of couples, often fusional, that led their perpetrators to commit one or more murders of unprecedented violence.

Contrary to popular belief, forged by many Hollywood productions featuring young killer couples driving at 100 miles an hour on the US freeways, statistically there are very few cases of serial murder involving husbands and wives. There are some famous duos, often linked by blood ties, such as Kenneth Bianchi and Angelo Buono, or Fred Waterfield and David Gore, even homosexual couples like Henry Lee Lucas and Ottis Toole, but rarely are the bonds of marriage strengthened by a sharing of victims. Married serial killers usually lead a highly compartmentalized double life, and almost never involve their partner in their criminal activities.

The nine cases I present to you in this book are exceptions. Some of them are quite infamous, but I have chosen to include them by adding some information that is not well known to the general public. I've also covered more obscure cases, like the Birnies in Australia, and the story of the Clark/Bundy couple; I think it's important to learn more about the dynamics behind these extraordinary unions.

We will see in these nine stories that they start with the meeting of a man prone to sexual sadism and a high sex drive, with a submissive, sometimes masochistic companion, who is also prone to pronounced sadistic tendencies. The sharing of violent fantasies, often in the form of confessions "on the pillow", takes an increasingly invasive place in the lovebirds' imagination. It is enough that both have already given in delinquency, even crime, for the moral barriers to collapse. Fantasy gives more and more room to scenarios of abductions that give way to elaborate plans, with assigned roles. The woman is often used as bait for her lover, like a lioness bringing a gazelle to its alpha male to devour it together.

You will see by reading these stories, the *modus operandi* are often strangely similar from one continent to another: kidnapping of hitchhikers in a vehicle, often a van. Repeated rapes, torture, killing, either in the vehicle or at home. Then the body is transported to a secluded place in the middle of the night, like a tissue discarded after use.

In these couples, women often present themselves as victims of the tyranny of a violent and perverse husband. Psychiatrists and judges are rarely duped, and these women face sentences as harsh as their partner. Prison often puts an end to the love that connects these abominable lovers. Most of the time, the trial is followed by a divorce.

Nonetheless, for us true crime lovers, these couples will always remain united in horror. There is no Michel Fourniret without Monique Olivier, no Charlie Starkweather without Caril Fugate. The history of crime will forever associate the names of these monstrous lovers, for the better, and especially the worst.

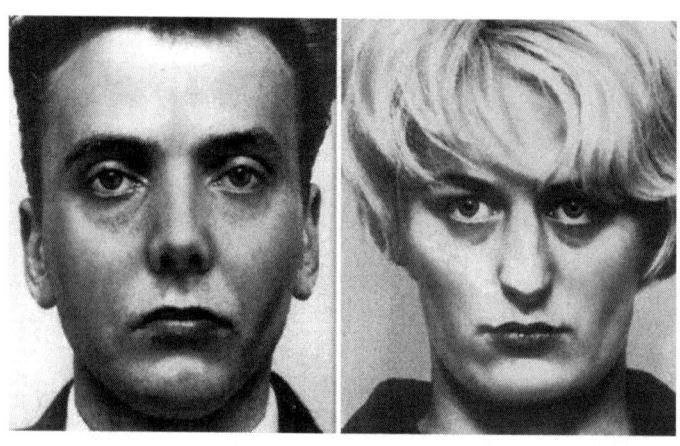

Ian Brady and Myra Hindley

The case of Ian Brady and Myra Hindley is one of the best-documented, and most widely followed, crime stories from the second half of the 20th century in the UK. This is understood by the age of their victims, adolescents and children, by the horror of the acts committed on them, but also by the fundamentally "monstrous" nature of their personalities, and their fascination with evil in all its forms, whether literary or political.

The true extent of the crimes committed by the couple was revealed only in 1985, when they finally resolved to confess their crimes, years after having proclaimed their innocence. The following story is based on what transpired from these confessions, but it goes without saying that it is quite possible that Myra Hindley had a much more active part in the murders than she suggested to her interlocutors from the judicial system and prison.

The setting of the crimes of the cursed couple is particularly sinister. These are moors located in the greater Manchester suburb, the Saddleworth Moor. It is a wet, desolate landscape dotted with bogs and moss sphagnum. It is in this gloomy environment that the couple buried four of their five known victims, sometimes taking pictures above their shallow graves.

Their first victim was Pauline Reade, a 16-year-old neighbor of Myra Hindley, who disappeared at a British Railways Club ball in Gorton on 12 July 1963. That night, Brady told Hindley he wanted to commit the "*perfect crime*". He was obsessed with the case of Leopold and Loeb, two wealthy American teenagers who murdered a 14-year-old boy to prove their "*intellectual superiority.*" Brady asked Hindley to drive their van while he followed her on a motorcycle; as soon as he spotted the ideal victim, Brady would signal Hindley to stop and pick up the person in question.

While driving down Gorton Lane, Brady saw a young girl walking down the street, and signaled Hindley to stop, which she did just after passing her. But when Brady asked Myra why she hadn't offered their prey to climb on board, his partner replied that she had recognized her. It was Marie Ruck, a neighbor of her mother.

Shortly after 8:00 p.m., continuing to drive on Froxmer Street, Brady spotted a girl dressed in a blue coat and signaled the van to stop. Hindley recognized Pauline Reade, a friend of her younger sister, Maureen. The girl agreed to get into the vehicle with Hindley, who asked her to help her find a glove she lost in the Saddleworth Moor. Reade agreed to help her.

At 16, Pauline Reade was older than Marie Ruck, and Hindley believed her disappearance would make less of a splash than that of a seven- or eight-year-old girl. When the van arrived on the moor, Hindley stopped, and Brady arrived shortly after on a motorcycle. Myra introduced the man to Reade as her boyfriend, explaining that he would help them find the glove. Brady took Reade into the moor while Hindley waited in the van.

About 30 minutes later, Brady returned alone and drove Hindley to the scene of the crime to see Pauline Reade's body lying on the ground, her throat cut. Then he told his companion to wait there while he looked for a suitable place to bury the girl. Hindley, seeing the clothes of the teenager in disarray, realized that Pauline was raped before being killed. She asked her lover if he had abused her, and he replied: *"Of course"*. On their way back, the couple hid the motorcycle inside the van and on the way home they met Pauline's mother, Joan, accompanied by her son Paul, they were looking for her in the street. Later, during his incarceration, Brady would claim that Hindley helped him kill the teenager, and also participated in her rape.

Four months later, accompanied by Brady, Hindley accosted 12-year-old John Kilbride early on the evening of 23 November 1963 at a market in Ashton, and they offered to accompany him under the pretext that his parents would be worried for him if he came home too late. Encouraged by the promise to taste a bottle of sherry, Kilbride accepted the offer and rode in the Ford Anglia that Hindley had rented. Brady told Kilbride that the sherry was at their house, and they would have to make a little detour to pick it up. On the way, he suggested making an additional stop to fetch a glove that Hindley lost in the moor, using the same ploy employed with Pauline Reade.

When they arrived at their destination, Brady took the boy with him while Hindley waited in the car. Brady raped Kilbride and tried to slit his throat before strangling him with a shoelace. Some time later, Brady would return to the exact place where he buried him to take pictures of Myra with their dog Puppet. In this photo, we can see the pile of earth that covers the grave.

Keith Bennett, 12, disappeared on his way to his grandmother's house in Longsight on 16 June 1964, four days after his birthday. Myra Hindley got him in their mini-pick-up (while Brady was sitting in the back) to help him load heavy boxes, promising to take him home. After taking him to the moor, Brady went with Bennett, probably in search of the famous glove. Hindley waited patiently, and after about half an hour, Brady reappeared alone once again, holding a shovel he had hidden at the location a few days earlier. When Hindley asked him how he killed the boy, Brady said that he raped him and then strangled him with a piece of rope.

Brady and Hindley went to a fair on December 26, 1964, looking for another victim, and noticed Lesley

Ann Downey, 10. When they realized that she was alone, they asked her to help them carry bags to their car. Once she was locked in the vehicle, they took her home and the girl was stripped, tied up and forced to pose for pornographic photos before being raped and finally killed, perhaps strangled with a rope. Hindley later stated that she had gone to prepare a bath for the girl and that she was already dead (allegedly killed by Brady) when she returned. In Chris Cowley's book *Face to Face with Evil: Conversations with Ian Brady*, Brady claims that it was Hindley who killed Lesley Ann Downey. The next morning, they drove the child's body to Saddleworth Moor, where she was buried completely naked, her clothes laid at her feet.

Brady's intention was to bribe a third partner, in order to help him commit more murders and robberies. Hindley's brother-in-law, 17-year-old David Smith, husband of Hindley's younger sister Maureen, would witness the next murder. Hindley's family did not approve of the marriage between Maureen and Smith, who had several criminal records. Over the previous year, Brady had befriended Smith, becoming closer and closer to the boy, which had worried Hindley, because the involvement of a third person could compromise their *"career"* as serial killers. Incidentally, Smith had a brief affair with Pauline Reade, the first victim of the *"Moors Murderers."*

On the evening of 6 October 1965, Hindley took Brady to the Manchester station, where she waited in the car while her lover chose a new victim; after a few minutes, Brady reappeared with Edward Evans,

FOLIE À DEUX

Brady and Hindley liked to take pictures of themselves
near the the graves of their victims.

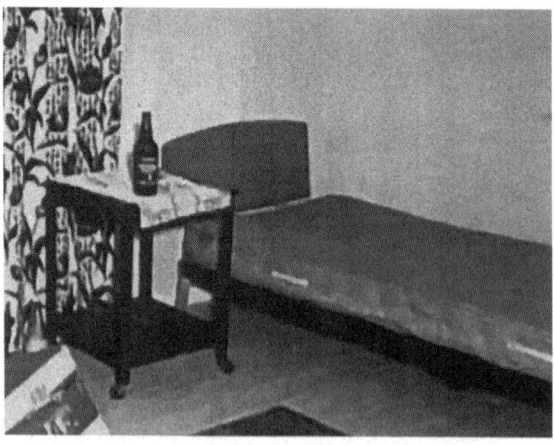

The bed where Leslie Ann Downey's murder took place.

introducing Hindley to him as his sister. After driving him home and relaxing over a bottle of wine, Brady asked Hindley to fetch her brother-in-law. Hindley told Smith to wait outside until she gave the signal, which was to turn on a light. At the agreed signal, Smith knocked on the door and was greeted by Brady, who asked him if he was coming for the *"mignonettes"*. Brady took Smith into the kitchen and left him there, telling him he was going to get the wine. A few minutes later, Smith heard a scream, followed by the cries of Hindley, who called him to help them. Smith entered the living room and saw Brady repeatedly hitting Evans with an axe, then strangling him with an electric cable. Evans' body was too heavy to carry in the car for Brady, who had sprained his ankle during the fight. He then asked Smith to put the body in a plastic bag and drag it into the guest room.

Smith agreed to meet with Brady the next night to help him get rid of Evans' body, but on his way home he woke up his wife and told her the whole story. Maureen told him that he must absolutely call the police. Three hours later, the couple called the nearest police station from a phone booth. According to the police report, Smith said, *"I waited about a minute or two, then suddenly I heard a hell of a scream; it sounded like a woman, really high-pitched. Then the screams carried on, one after another, really loud. Then I heard Myra shout, "Dave, help him," very loud. When I ran in, I just stood inside the living room, and I saw a young lad. He was lying with his head and shoulders on the couch and his legs were on the floor. He was facing upwards. Ian was standing over him, facing him, with his legs on either*

side of the young lad's legs. The lad was still screaming ...
Ian had a hatchet in his hand ... he was holding it above
his head, and he hit the lad on the left side of his head
with the hatchet. I heard the blow, it was a terrible hard
blow, it sounded horrible."

These are the facts. What more can we say to understand the dynamics of the world's most infamous killer couple? For this, we must go back to their childhood and their encounter.

Ian Duncan Stewart was born on 2 January 1938 in Glasgow, Scotland, to 28-year-old single mother Maggie Stewart. Brady's father is unknown, although his mother claimed he was a journalist for a Glasgow newspaper, who died three months before Ian was born. Stewart did not receive much help from her family, and after only a few months she was forced to give her baby to Mary and John Sloan, a couple who already had four children. Ian took the foster family's name, and was called Ian Sloan. His mother continued to visit him throughout his childhood.

A few months later, the family moved to Pollok, a small rural town in the suburbs of Glasgow. He was admitted to Shawlands Academy, a school for above-average students.

At Shawlands, the young man's behavior began to deteriorate; as a teenager he was arrested twice for burglary. He left school at 15 and started working as a waiter in Govan. Nine months later, he was hired as a butcher boy. He had a girlfriend, Evelyn Grant, but their relationship ended when Ian threatened her with a knife after an argument motivated by his jealousy. He then committed other crimes, with a total of nine counts, and shortly before his seventeenth birthday, he was released on parole, with the obligation to live with his birth mother. At the time, she had moved to Manchester and married an Irish fruit merchant named Patrick Brady. The man forced Ian to work with him at the market.

A year after moving to Manchester, Brady was arrested again for theft. The boy spent three months in Strangeways juvenile prison, then he was transferred to Latchmere House prison in London, and finally to the Hatfield correctional home in Yorkshire. After being caught drunk, Ian was transferred to a harder-than-usual prison in the city of Hull.

Released on 14 November 1957, Brady returned to Manchester, where he lived by expedients. Determined to "*improve intellectually*", he began studying accounting as a self-taught student at the public library. He took his family and friends by surprise by staying in his room for hours at a time to study.

In January 1959, Brady found a job at a chemical distribution company based in Gorton. He became passionate about reading Adolf Hitler's *Mein Kampf*, and his interest in Nazism in general became a concern. He bought a Triumph Tiger Cub motorcycle, with which he often took long trips to the countryside.

FOLIE À DEUX

In 1961, he met Myra Hindley, 19, and they became engaged after just a few months of dating.

Myra Hindley was born on 23 July 1942 in Gorton, a working-class suburb of Manchester. Her parents, Nellie and Bob Hindley (the latter an alcoholic), beat her regularly when she was a child. The little house where the family lived was so miserable that Myra and her parents all stayed in the only clean room, the little girl sleeping in a cot next to the double bed. The family's living conditions worsened with the birth in 1946 of Myra's younger sister, Maureen. Shortly after her birth, Hindley, then 5 years old, was sent to live with her grandmother, who lived nearby.

Hindley's father had fought in North Africa, Cyprus and Italy during the Second World War as a paratrooper. Under arms, he was known as a "tough guy" and he expected that this combative character would also be present in his daughter; he often urged her to fight, emphasizing that she "must learn to fend for herself". When Hindley was eight, a boy from the block scratched her face, making her bleed. The little girl burst into tears and ran to her parents' house, where she fell on her father, who reprimanded her and threatened to beat her if she did not seek revenge. Myra eventually found the boy and punched him, as her father had taught her.

Malcolm MacCulloch, a professor of forensic psychiatry at the University of Cardiff, suggests that this particular episode and the role played by Hindley's

Brady and Hindley idolized
the Marquis de Sade and Adolf Hitler.

father are "the keystone" to understand Hindley's role in the "Moors murders":

"Her relationship with her father was brutal. Not only was she beaten at home, but she was encouraged to be violent. When it happens at a young age, it can cause personality impairment with lasting effects."

One of her closest friends was 13-year-old Michael Higgins, who lived on a nearby street. In June 1957, he invited her to go swimming with other friends in a disused pool. Hindley, a good swimmer, chose not to go, preferring to date a friend, Pat Jepson. Higgins drowned in the pool, and - once she learned of the drama - Hindley felt strongly guilty for leaving him alone that day.

Hindley got her first job in an electrical equipment company. Around the same time, she had a brief romantic relationship with a young man named Ronnie Sinclair and when she turned 17, they became engaged. The engagement didn't last long, as Myra thought Ronnie was too immature to start a family with her.

Shortly after her seventeenth birthday, Myra dyed her hair for the first time. She took judo classes once a week, but it was hard to find people who wanted to train with her because she fought too hard. She found another job at Bratby & Hinchliffe, an engineering firm in Gorton, but was fired after six months for absenteeism.

In 1961, 19-year-old Myra Hindley met Ian Brady and fell in love with him when she knew he had a criminal record. She began to keep a diary and, although she also dated other men, the pages of the diary clearly showed her fascination with Brady, with whom she first spoke on 27 July 1961. On 22 December, Brady offered to accompany her to the cinema, and the young couple went to see the biblical film *The King of Kings*. Their appointments soon took on a regular rhythm; evening at the cinema to go see films forbidden to minors, then dinner at Hindley's, and more after a few glasses of wine. Brady gave his girlfriend books to study, and the couple often spent their lunch breaks reading aloud books about Nazi atrocities.

Hindley tried to marry the Aryan look by dyeing her hair platinum blonde. She also changed her way of dressing, starting to wear black leather boots and jackets. The couple regularly visited the local library, borrowing books on philosophy, criminology and torture history. They also read the works of the Marquis de Sade, and *Crime and Punishment* by Fyodor Dostoyevsky. Although she was not an experienced driver (she had only obtained her driving license on the third attempt, in 1963), Hindley often drove a van, with which both lovers wanted to rob a bank. Brady and Hindley's criminal plans failed, but their interest in violent pornography grew over the weeks. These fantasies turned into little desires of murders, with the consequences that we know.

After Evans' murder, and Smith's call to the police, two investigators went to Hindley's house, and found the victim's body in the couple's room. Brady was arrested, commenting simply, "Eddie and I had a disagreement, and things got out of hand."

On 11 October, it was Myra's turn to be arrested. Police found a schoolbook belonging to John Kilbride in her home. In custody, Smith mentioned that Brady had left a suitcase at a locker at the Manchester station. The detectives found the luggage and when they opened it, they were confronted with pornographic photographs showing a very young girl, as well as the audio recording of her torment. They showed the "least shocking" photos to Lesley's mother, Ann Downey, who instantly acknowledged her daughter as missing for a year.

A girl from the neighborhood explained to the police that the couple sometimes took her to the Saddleworth moors. An initial search revealed the remains of Downey. Kilbride's body was found shortly afterwards, thanks to photos of the moors found in the suitcase, indicating the places of some burials.

At first, the couple denied killing the children. They were nevertheless charged with three murders on 6 December 1965. The trial opened on 19 April 1966 and after two weeks of hearings, Brady and Hindley were sentenced to life in prison. Reporters covering the trial described Brady's coldness and arrogance. When the audio of Downey's ordeal was broadcast on loudspeakers in the courtroom, the room froze. Hindley claimed she was in another room while Brady took the pictures of the little girl, but she could not convince anyone.

There is a particular fact about the "Moors Murderers". Unlike other murders committed by famous serial killers, the crimes of Brady and Hindley became more spread-out over time, after an initial frenzy. It was almost a year between the murder of Leslie Ann Downey and that of Edward Evans. Some observers believe that this delay is due to the fact that the couple took a photo and recorded the little girl's cries, which may have served to vent their death-seeking impulses in the meantime. According to the transcriptions, the little girl cries and begs the two torturers to let her see her mother, while Christmas music plays in the background. In his autobiography, Detective Topping, who interviewed Hindley, recounts what she told him about the recording: "[She spoke] *of Lesley Ann Downey's recordings. Contrary to popular belief, the tapes were recorded while photographs were taken - not during the torture session. She denied that Lesley Ann had been subjected to physical torture. After evaluating the evidence at the trial and listening to the recordings, I did find that they were made while photos were being taken; But I told Hindley to deprive a child of her mother, and then strip her, tie her up and gag her, which I think was a form of torture...even though it wasn't the kind of torture that we usually think of.*"

Another question often asked about Ian Brady is his victimology. Why attack children when he had never shown a particular inclination for pedophilia? The answer will shock more than one.

Dr Alan Keightley, a West Midlands professor, befriended Brady during his detention. He visited the psychopath at Ashworth Psychiatric Hospital every month and corresponded with him regularly.

One day, Dr. Keightley asked Brady why he was targeting children. Brady replied without blinking an eye that he had wanted to engage in "existential exercises", that is to say, he wanted to test his theory that he was free to live as he saw fit by testing the limits of his free will. He tried to explain his reasoning to him as follows: "My dark concerns led me to the path of pure existentialism, where the will to dare everything and suffer the consequences became paramount." He even added, "People who lead a conventional, boring and dreary life are the ones who are crazy."

Brady served his sentence in solitary confinement in various English prisons before being diagnosed as a "psychopath" by a psychiatrist, which earned him a transfer to the Ashworth Dangerous Patient Unit in November 1985. That same year he confessed to a reporter from the *Sunday People* that he had also killed Reade and Bennett. Later, Hindley received a letter from Bennett's mother, imploring her to point out where his son's grave was, which she agreed to do. The police escorted England's most famous prisoner into the moors, mobilizing more than 200 people to help with the searches. This visit ended in a fiasco; no graves being found. It took several months before the police finally found Reade's body, 100 meters from the location of Downey's grave. This prompted Brady to cooperate in his turn with the search. He too was escorted to the site, by helicopter, but no other body was found.

In the following years, huge efforts were made by the Manchester police to find Bennett's body; among other things, an American satellite can detect traces of earthworks in the ground. To this day, many amateur investigators continue to roam this sinister territory in search of bone fragments.

In 2001, Brady wrote *The Gates of Janus*, an analysis of crimes committed by other serial killers, including Peter Sutcliffe and Graham Young, whom he had met in prison. Kilbride's family called for a boycott of the book, but it was published in the US by independent publisher Feral House. Its owner, Adam Parfrey, made this statement to the BBC:

"It was the British tabloids that made me know Ian Brady. I started to wonder why this guy was the subject of forty years of continuous and obsessive media coverage, Using the kind of terminology reserved for enemies in holy wars. Many other criminals have killed children, and almost all are forgotten, but not Ian Brady. Why? What's the best way to talk about the horror of Ian Brady's crimes? By reading tabloids? Or by looking at the crimes in a more clinical and realistic way?

This may be a Jungian remark, but human behavior cannot be tackled, and its malignity reduced by reacting in a simplistic way to it and acting with more hatred and aggression. I understand and appreciate the determination of some victims to want to ban the sale of this book, but I think limiting our ability to understand the thoughts and motives of criminals is not helping us.

The Saddleworth Moors were the subject of dozens
of searches for the victims' remains.

It is in the editorial line of Feral House to explore sociological extremes, as with my own book, Apocalypse Culture. And although we have published a lot of books that provoke reflection on difficult topics, The Gates of Janus is one of the most difficult to defend.

I have already received a lot of hate mail. How can I dare to publish such a book? Why promote the work of a child murderer? People don't understand that publishing a book that sells a few thousand copies and seriously analyzes the behavior of criminals is not the same as making an apology of these crimes. The tabloids themselves, who sell hundreds of thousands of copies, are the ones who cynically profit most from these crimes."

In 1987, the Manchester city council had the house where some of the crimes of Brady and Hindley were committed destroyed.

Hindley died on 15 November 2002 at the age of 60 from pneumonia due to excessive smoking. Ironically, her ashes were scattered in a park located 10 miles away from the Saddleworth Moors.

After several hunger strikes, Brady died on 15 May 2017 in Ashworth of *"natural causes"*. His ashes were scattered into the sea.

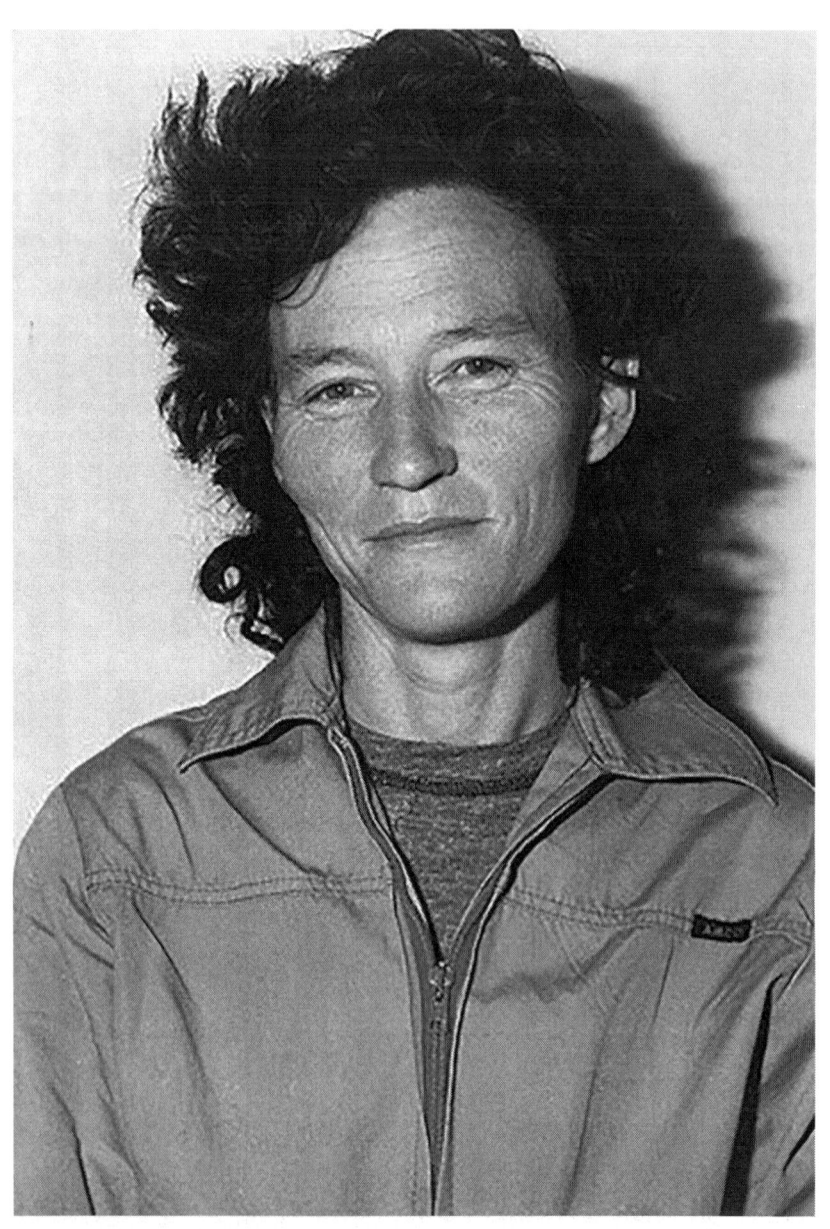

David and Catherine Birnie

It was by far the worst house on the street, and the only good thing that could be said about it was that it made the other houses around it look like palaces.

Yet this ungrateful home would one day become the most famous house in Australia. In the years to come, people would slow down and point their fingers at her as they drove past. It would become as famous for the Australians as Jeffrey Dahmer's apartment 213 in Milwaukee, or 10 Rillington Place and 25 Cromwell Street in England.

Before becoming so infamous, the house at number 3 Moorhouse Street in Willagee, on the outskirts of Perth, was the residence, the love nest, the prison and death row of Catherine and David Birnie, a married serial killer couple, the only one of its kind in this part of the world. It is there that they committed the worst atrocities against their young victims.

The Birnies were not particularly selective about who they killed, since their victims were typically female and between 15 and 30 years old. Whenever the Birnies wanted to kill a girl, they would drive along the roads of Perth and take hitchhikers, common at the time in Australia.

Their victims could not be suspicious of this friendly-looking couple, until it was too late. At the tip of a knife, they would take them back to Moorhouse Street and lock them up there for the time they had to fulfill their depraved sexual fantasies. Once they were full of sex and violence, they would murder them without hesitation. The lucky ones were first anesthetized with an overdose of sleeping pills, then strangled. Others were stabbed or beaten to death with a knife or axe while sitting in shallow graves dug for the occasion in a pine forest secluded a few minutes' drive from Perth.

On November 5, 1986, Detective Paul Ferguson made public at a press conference that he suspected there was a serial killer on the loose in the area when Denise Karen Brown, 21, was reported missing. Denise was the fourth young woman in the region to go missing in 27 days. This kind of thing just didn't happen in Perth, one of the most isolated cities in the world, on the west coast of Australia. In other big Australian cities like Sydney or Melbourne, this kind of thing could happen, but surely not in Perth.

All the missing women came from good families, and it was extremely unlikely that they had run away without a valid reason. Ferguson had eliminated all possibilities of connection between the missing women, and he had followed up on possible secret boyfriends, married lovers or hidden drug problems that could explain this situation. But it was in vain, and they had to face the evidence: all these disappearances were extremely worrying.

Ferguson's instinct, inspired by years of experience, was that there was a serial killer on the loose, a criminal who had mastered the art of kidnapping young women without witnesses. What intrigued detective Ferguson most was that two of the women had not completely disappeared, because their friends and relatives had received letters and phone calls from them after they were reported missing.

Susannah Candy, 15, had mailed two letters to her parents, one from Perth and the other from nearby Fremantle Harbor, in the first two weeks after she disappeared. The two letters said she was fine and would soon be home. And Denise Brown had called a girlfriend the day after her "runaway" to tell her that everything was fine. After that, no one had heard from her.

Ferguson consulted a former CIB chief, Bill Neilson, who agreed with his theory of the serial killer. And if anyone knew anything about it, it was him. Bill Neilson had been in charge of tracking down another Perth serial killer, Eric Edgar Cooke, a truck driver who killed six people and possibly two others in the early 1960s. Neilson had brought him to justice and had seen Cooke swing on a rope at Fremantle Prison in 1964.

On November 10th, five days after the disappearance of Denise Brown, Detective Inspector Ferguson and Detective Sergeant Vince Katich were following up on the young woman's disappearance when they had the breakthrough they were desperately waiting for. They were told by radio that a young half-naked woman had just broken into a small commercial complex in Willagee and was taken to the Palmyra police station.

Believing it to be Denise Brown, Ferguson and Katich rushed to the police station. Instead, they were confronted by a 16-year-old girl who told them an incredible story. The terrified teenager told them that she had been kidnapped at knifepoint the day before by a man and a woman who had asked her for directions as she walked along the street near her house in the Nedlands district.

She had been taken to a house in Willagee where the couple tore off all her clothes before tying her to a bed by her hands and feet. The girl told the detectives that the man raped her several times while the woman watched. The couple had mentioned injecting cocaine into the man's penis.

The next morning, when the man left for work, the woman released the girl and forced her to call her parents to tell them that she was at a friend's house and that she was fine. While she was using the phone, she managed to write down the number on the handset.

When the woman left the room to go and open the front door, presumably to let a cocaine dealer in, the girl climbed out of an open window and escaped from the place of her martyrdom. She was able to give the police a full description of her attackers, along with their phone number and address.

When she told Detectives Ferguson and Katich about the phone call that she had been forced to make to her parents, they immediately understood that this couple was perhaps to be the kidnappers of the two young women who disappeared earlier.

Moreover, there was no doubt in their minds that the fact that the girl was allowed to see the faces of the couple and where they lived, meant they were planning to kill her once they were done with her. If so, it was very likely that the couple had already killed before, perhaps several times.

The girl led the team of investigators to the white brick house on Moorhouse Street. There was no one inside. Two detectives hid in a van parked in the driveway and eventually got their hands on Catherine Margaret Birnie. She told them without difficulty where to find her husband. Minutes later, other police officers stopped David John Birnie at the garage where he worked.

The Birnies vigorously denied the girl's allegations. Instead, they claimed that she had been there of her own free will to share a marijuana bong with them. David admitted having sex with the girl but claimed that he did not rape her. A search of the house allowed detectives to find the victim's bag and a pack of cigarettes that she had the good sense to hide in the ceiling as proof that it had indeed been there, sequestered, but there wasn't much else to prove the rape allegation or link the Birnies to the other missing women.

Knowing they needed a confession to confirm their suspicions, Ferguson and Katich hoped that under intense interrogation, one of the Birnies would crack and admit to at least the girl's rape. It was her word against theirs. Ferguson and Katich questioned the couple separately. Against all odds, it was David Birnie who finally cracked first.

Just after 7:00 that evening, Detective Sergeant Katich escorted David Birnie to the place where he claimed he had buried victims. Joking, speaking of the missing women, Birnie exclaimed, "It's dark. Better to take the shovel and good lamps to dig them up." The convoy rode along the road to Wanneroo, through a pine forest. Birnie seemed relaxed and he talked so much that they had almost reached the next town before he realized they had gone too far. He asked them to turn around. On the way, peering into the darkness, David Birnie recognized a trail that led off the highway into the pine plantation of Gnangara.

About 400 meters into the forest, Birnie asked them to stop. He pointed to a mound of sand. "Dig there," he said. Within minutes, police had found the body of Denise Karen Brown, reported missing only five days earlier.

The Birnies were arrested in 1986.

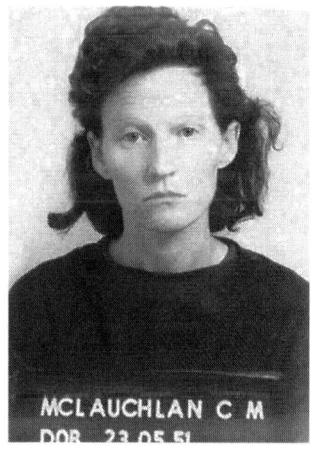

Leaving a policeman at the site, Birnie led the convoy south to the Gleneagle picnic area near Armadale. After driving for half an hour, Birnie led the police through the forest along a narrow track. On a slope about 40 meters from the track, police discovered the decaying body of 22-year-old Mary Frances Neilson, who had disappeared on October 6.

One kilometer away on the track, David Birnie pointed out to them the burial place of 15-year-old Susannah Candy, who had been missing since October 19.

Then Catherine Birnie told them that it was her turn. She wanted to tell them the position of the next tomb. She told them that it was there that they had buried Noelene Patterson, 31, who they had kidnapped and murdered on October 30.

Catherine went to great lengths to explain to the police that she had hated Noelene since she and David had taken her. She was happy that she died. As she showed the police the grave, she spat on it. She was very proud to be able to find the grave without help. It was as if she didn't want David to get all the credit.

Leaving the burial site, David Birnie told Katich, "What a waste of young lives." But Katich was surprised that none of the Birnies showed emotion or embarrassment while the bodies were being discovered. On the contrary, they seemed to enjoy being the center of attention when they pointed out the graves to the police. There was absolutely no doubt in the inspector's mind that if the girl had not escaped earlier in the day, the killings would have continued.

The psychiatrists involved in the case agreed to emphasize that Catherine Birnie could not have killed alone. She didn't have the shoulders. But this mother of six was totally obsessed with David Birnie and would do anything for him, including killing. She was even willing to kill herself for him. When he was attached to one of their victims, Catherine said she would rather die by her own hand than see him fall in love with someone else.

David John Birnie was the eldest of six children. Margaret and John Birnie, his parents, did their best for their children, but times were hard. David Birnie's parents were known for their chronic alcoholism. Throughout their youth, social services often took their children away from them and placed them in government institutions.

At the time of the murders, David Birnie's mother was living in poverty. His little apartment was full of food scraps, dirty dishes, filled ashtrays and broken furniture. The place was covered with dust and dirt. She had lost hope years ago and hadn't seen her eldest son in years. David's father died in 1986 after a long illness.

Catherine and David first met when they were children, when their families lived next to each other. Catherine's life was miserable. Her mother died when she was ten months old, and the child was sent to live in South Africa with her father. She was sent back to Australia after two years and raised by her grandparents. She was a sad little girl who rarely smiled, had no friends. Other children were not allowed to play with her.

David Birnie started dating Catherine when they were teenagers. David already had a well-stocked record for several offences. The only time he proved that he could do something constructive was in the early 1960s, when he took a jockey apprenticeship.

But like most things in David Birnie's life, it didn't last very long. Coach Eric Parnham remembers Birnie as a pale, sickly boy to whom he gave this job out of compassion. Birnie had been recommended to him as an apprentice, but when he went to fetch him from his house, he found that it was a slum guarded by a pack of dogs. Despite this first unfavorable impression, Birnie worked in his stables for almost a year, and he seemed on track to become a good jockey.

Parnham eventually fired him when the young man was accused of assaulting and robbing an elderly person. Fortunately, Catherine had become infatuated with Birnie at that time of her life. She did whatever he wanted and together they committed a crime that sent them both to prison.

On 11 June 1969, David and Catherine pleaded guilty before the Perth Police Court to eleven counts of burglary and theft of goods worth nearly $3,000. Catherine was pregnant with another man's child.

They admitted the fact that they stole a blowtorch and used it to try to open a safe at the drive-in on Waverley. Catherine received a suspended sentence and Birnie was sent to detention for nine months.

On 9 July 1969, they were tried by the Supreme Court for eight other counts of burglary and robbery. They pleaded guilty and David was sentenced to three more years in prison. Catherine was given four years with additional conditional sentence.

On 21 June 1970, David escaped from Karnet prison and teamed up with Catherine again. When they were apprehended on 10 July, they were charged with 53 counts of robbery, burglary, motor vehicle driving and car theft. The police found clothes, wigs, bedding, radios, food, books, 100 plastic sticks, 120 detonators and three fuses. Catherine admitted that she knew she had done wrong, but she also said that she loved David so much that there was nothing she would not do for him. She was going to prove it in a particularly sordid way in the years to come.

David Birnie was sentenced to two and a half years in prison, and Catherine to six months. Her newborn baby was taken from her by social workers and placed in foster care until her release. Out of prison a few months later, and away from the bad influence of David Birnie, Catherine was hired as a servant for a family based in Fremantle.

For the first time in her life, the skinny young woman seemed to have found some peace and happiness.

Donald McLaughlan, the son of the family she worked for, fell in love with her and they married on 31 May 1972. It was also Catherine's 21st birthday. Shortly after, she gave birth to the first of their six children. They named the little boy "Little Donny" in honor of his father. Seven months later, Little Donny was hit by a car in front of his mother. Psychiatrists later stressed the importance of this tragedy in the horrors to come.

Meanwhile, her marriage seemed to be falling apart, as Catherine had fallen in love with David Birnie again.

No one was surprised when she left the conjugal home. The family lived in a State Housing Commission house in the working-class suburb of Victoria Park. Catherine had to look after her unemployed husband, their six children, her father and uncle. Her home looked like a pigsty. She was not proud of the cleanliness of her children or the house. There was never money to feed herself. One day, she phoned her husband to tell him that she would not return.

Behind his back, she had been dating David Birnie for the previous two years and was returning to live with him. After thirteen years of this insipid married life, she moved in with her first love. Although they never married, Catherine changed her name to Birnie, and she became his common-law partner.

But the Birnie family was far from normal. David Birnie's sexual appetite seemed insatiable. David's younger brother, James Birnie, lived with the couple for a short time when he was released from prison after serving five months for touching his six-year-old niece. He told a journalist, "When I left prison, I had nowhere to go. I couldn't go back to my mother's house because I had assaulted her, and she had a restraining order against me. I got into a fight with Mom and the police kicked me out. Mom has a drinking problem, so David and Catherine let me move in. They were not right. David kept saying that he was going to kill me to freak me out."

David Birnie had few friends, was obsessed with sexual perversions, and had a large collection of pornographic videos. "He needs to have sex four or five times a day," James Birnie later said of his brother. "I saw him use a syringe full of that substance that you get when they stitch you up. It makes you numb. He put the needle in his penis, then he had sex with his girlfriend. David had a lot of women. He's always with someone different."

The murders started in 1986. David and Catherine Birnie had tried everything sexually together and they wanted to experience new chills. They started talking about kidnapping and rape. David tried to persuade his accomplice by telling her that she would reach incredible orgasms by watching him penetrate another bound and gagged woman. Catherine, far from being offended, seemed to be excited by this idea.

Their first opportunity came on October 6, 1986, when 22-year-old student Mary Neilson showed up at the Birnies' home to buy car tires. She had seen Birnie at his work in the garage and he had then suggested to him to go to his house so that he would give a discount to her.

Mary was studying psychology at the University of Western Australia and worked part-time in a suburban deli. She hoped to be a counsellor in the Community Welfare Department. Her parents were both teachers and were on vacation in the UK when their daughter disappeared.

Mary was last seen leaving the shop on Monday, October 6, to attend a conference at the university. But she never arrived. Her Mitsubishi Galant sedan was found six days later in a car park on the riverbank, opposite the central police station. David Birnie had driven her there. It was as if he had deliberately left a clue for the police.

As Mary Neilson entered Birnie's house, he threatened her with a knife, licked her, gagged her and chained her to bed. Catherine Birnie watched her lover rape the girl several times. She then asked him about what had made him most excited. That way, she would know what to do next time to please him.

Catherine knew that Mary Neilson would eventually die, but she and Birnie had not yet discussed it. That night, they took the girl to Gleneagle National Park where David raped her again, then he wrapped a nylon rope around her neck and slowly clamped her with a tree branch, like a turnstile.

The four victims of the Birnies' house of horrors.

Mary Neilson choked at his feet, then he stabbed her body and buried her in a shallow grave. He explained to Catherine that the knife wounds would allow gas to escape when the body decomposes. He had read it somewhere in a book.

The second murder took place two weeks later, when they abducted 15-year-old Susannah Candy while hitchhiking along the Stirling Highway in Claremont.

An outstanding student at Hollywood High School, Susannah lived in Nedlands with her parents, two brothers and a sister. Her father was one of the best eye surgeons in Western Australia. The couple had been driving for hours looking for a victim when they spotted Susannah. Seconds after getting into the car, she had a knife to her throat and her hands were tied. She was taken back to their home in Willagee where she was gagged, chained to the bed and raped.

After Birnie had finished subjecting his victim to abuse, Catherine Birnie went to bed with them. She knew how much it excited her lover. When he was finished, David Birnie tried to strangle the girl with the nylon rope, but she became hysterical and began to struggle violently. The Birnies forced her to swallow sleeping pills to calm her down. Once Susannah was asleep, David put the rope around her neck and asked Catherine to prove how much her love for him was unwavering by killing her.

Catherine agreed willingly. She slowly tightened the rope around the girl's neck until she stopped breathing.

David Birnie stood by the bed and watched her do it. When asked later why she had done it, Catherine replied, "Because I wanted to see how strong I was in my inner self. I felt nothing. It was as I expected. I was ready to follow him to the ends of the earth and do everything possible to satisfy his desires. This girl was a female. Females hurt and destroy males."

They buried Susannah Candy near the grave of Mary Neilson in the forest.

On November 1, the hellish couple saw 31-year-old Noelene Patterson standing beside her car on the Canning Highway in East Fremantle. She ran out of gas on the way home from her bartending job at the Nedlands Golf Club.

Noelene lived with her mother in the peaceful suburb of Bicton, on the banks of the Swan River. She was an extremely popular woman, and the club members described her as charming and polite. She had been a stewardess at Ansett Airlines for nine years and had worked for magnate Alan Bond as a stewardess on his private jet for two years. Noelene had been working at the golf club for about a year when she agreed to ride in the Birnies' vehicle.

Noelene did not hesitate to climb in, judging for herself from the friendly smiles that the couple, who were apparently harmless, gave her. Gross mistake: once inside, she found herself very quickly with a knife under her throat, her hands were tied, and the driver ordered her not to move or she would be gutted on the spot. She was taken back to Moorhouse Street where David raped her several times after gagging and chaining her to bed.

Catherine Birnie hated Noelene Patterson from the moment she got her in the car. Beautiful and elegant, Noelene was everything Catherine wanted to be. What's more, David seemed particularly attracted to her. They had originally decided to kill Noelene Patterson that night, but when David started wanting to push the deadline, Catherine became furious. She felt that she was losing her man. At one point, she put the tip of a knife against her heart and threatened to kill herself unless he chose one of them.

David Birnie kept Noelene prisoner in the house for three days before Catherine insisted that he kill her. He gave her a large dose of sleeping pills and strangled her under the watchful eye of his companion, while she slept. They took her body to the forest and buried her with the others. Catherine Birnie later admitted that at this moment she felt a certain pleasure in throwing shovels of sand on the face of the dead woman.

On 5 November, they kidnapped 21-year-old Denise Brown while she was waiting for a bus on the Stirling Highway. Denise was a playful girl who worked as a part-time computer technician in Perth and spent most of her free time in the local nightclubs. She shared an apartment in Nedlands with her boyfriend and another couple. Denise spent her last night at the Coolbellup hotel with a friend. She agreed to be picked up by the Birnies as they left the Stoned Crow liquor store in

Fremantle. A close friend later said, "She was someone who did anything to help anyone. She trusted too many people. Maybe that's why she didn't hesitate to come aboard."

At the threat of a knife, Denise was taken to the Willagee house, chained to the bed and raped. The following afternoon, the couple took her to the Wanneroo pine plantation. On the way they almost picked up another victim. After the arrest of the Birnies, a 19-year-old student told the police how two people she later recognized as Catherine and David Birnie had offered to get into their vehicle.

After finishing her university classes, she was walking along Pinjar Road, Wanneroo, when a car stopped next to her. There were two people in the front and one person lying on the back seat. Later she realized that the person in the back was probably Denise Brown.

She told the police, "I felt uncomfortable. I didn't recognize the car. There was a man driving and a woman in the front seat. The man kept looking down, not looking at me and the woman was drinking a can of rum and cola. I thought it strange that she was drinking at this time of day. He didn't look at me once, the woman was talking. She asked me if I wanted them to take me somewhere. I said, "No, I don't live far." Then I looked at the back seat and saw a rather small person with short brown hair lying on the seat. I thought it was their son or daughter sleeping in the back. The person seemed to be sleeping and from the haircut, she looked like a boy but for some reason I felt it was a girl. I told them once again that I didn't need a ride because I like walking. The man looked up for the first time and looked me straight in the eye. At that time, other cars engaged in the street, and I started walking but they kept looking at me from their vehicle. Finally, the car started, and they made another U-turn and drove to Pinjar Road, towards the pine plantation. It was only when I saw a picture of Catherine Birnie that I realized who they were. I don't know what would have happened to me if I had gotten in that car."

Once out of sight in the forest, David Birnie raped Denise Brown while the couple waited for darkness. They then dragged the young woman out of the car and David attacked her again. In the light of Catherine's torch, Birnie stuck a knife into Denise's neck while he raped her.

Denise didn't die right away. Catherine Birnie, still holding the torch, found a larger knife and urged her lover to stab her again. He didn't need much encouragement. He beat her until Denise rolled around at his feet. Convinced that the girl was dead, they dug a shallow grave and laid the body there.

As they covered Denise Brown with dirt, she was caught in a final spasm and folded in half in her grave. Birnie grabbed an axe and struck her head with the flat side. When the girl collapsed under the impact, he turned the head of the axe and split her skull with the sharp side. The couple then finished covering her body with earth.

Catherine, on the other hand, was guilty of a certain latitude. She was beginning to wonder if it would be possible for her to let their next victim escape. She later told the police, "I think I had to make the decision that sooner or later, there was going to be an end to the carnage. I had reached the stage where I didn't know what to do. I was ready to give them a chance. I knew David would kill the next one too, and I probably made that decision that night. I was sick of all those murders. I thought if something didn't happen soon, it would go on forever. And in the back of my mind, there was another fear. I was very afraid of having to watch another murder like Denise Brown, the girl he killed with an axe. I wanted to avoid this at all costs, but deep down, I had reached the point where I really didn't care if the girl would escape or not. When I heard the last one had escaped, I felt a cold sweat running down my spine. I said, 'David will be furious. What do I tell him?'"

On 12 November 1986. David John Birnie and Catherine Margaret Birnie appeared before the Fremantle court to be read four counts of murder. The public was deeply indignant at the crimes committed by the couple and a crowd gathered in front of the court. The police were checking the bags of everyone who entered the building. The detention cell leading to the courtroom was heavily guarded by police.

David Birnie was taken to the courtroom in handcuffs to a police officer. Catherine Birnie, who was barefoot, was also handcuffed to a policeman and she wore blue jeans with a light brown plaid shirt.

They stood by while the charges against them were read aloud. Neither had a lawyer. Their request for bail was officially refused and the Birnies were placed in pre-trial detention until the trial.

When asked if she wanted to be held in custody for eight or 30 days before her next appearance in court, Catherine Birnie looked at her lover and replied: "I will go where he goes."

On 10 February 1987, a huge crowd gathered in front of the Supreme Court of Perth. When the Birnies arrived in a cell van, the crowd chanted, "Hang them!" Bill Power, a journalist who covered the crimes and Birnie's trial for the *Perth Daily News*, remembers Birnie's appearance at the Perth Supreme Court as one of the most frightening experiences in his career and he remembers it as if it was yesterday.

"*There was nothing distinctive about David and Catherine Birnie when they appeared in the box of the accused to face multiple charges of murdering young women. Missing in the streets of Perth,*" reports Bill in the newspaper columns. "*They were a rather ordinary couple that could be found running a gas station in a country town. David was a rather small man, and his wife Catherine was dull and a bit chubby; both were surrounded by policemen.*

David Birnie appeared first up the stairs leading to the detention cells located under the court and he seemed totally out of place in the very majestic Supreme Court of Perth. He sat on the bench, glancing at the police, the public present and the huge media contingent as Catherine walked up the stairs to the courtroom.

The skinny little serial killer was quite fascinating to watch, But nothing could have prepared me for the moment when Catherine Birnie appeared at the top of the stairs leading to the room where the accusations were to be read to them.

If you have ever seen a wild cat in a cage, try to imagine that same cat trapped in the enclosed spaces of a narrow staircase. Catherine Birnie fought like a raging woman against the guards charged with her escort and she screamed and vociferated insults until she reached the courtroom and spotted her well-beloved David. It was only then that she calmed down.

David Birnie then went to court to hear the murder charges against him, and Catherine was allowed to sit on a small wooden bench immediately behind him. As the judge listed the crimes against him, Birnie stood still with her hands joined behind her back."

"*What I witnessed next, I will carry to my grave,*" Power recalls. "*As the heinous charges of kidnapping, rape, torture and murder were laid against him, Catherine Birnie leaned forward, reached out her right hand and gently stroked David Birnie's hand behind his back. The Supreme Court of Western Australia has rarely seen such a strange expression of love.*"

David Birnie pleaded guilty to four counts of murder and one count of kidnapping and rape, sparing the families of his victims the agony of a lengthy trial. "That's the least I can do," he told one of the inspectors. Catherine Birnie was not forced to speak in court, as her lawyer was waiting for a psychiatric report to determine her mental health. She was dismissed for a later appearance that month.

"It was over in a matter of minutes," Power recalls. *"Sweet Catherine, who had shown such devotion to her husband a few moments earlier, was dragged out of the room by kicking, Screaming and spitting down the wooden staircase to a prison van waiting next to the courthouse. Perhaps she did not want another man than David to touch her."*

Justice Wallace sentenced David Birnie to the maximum sentence of life imprisonment with strict security measures. "The law is not strong enough to express the community's horror at this sadistic killer who tortured, raped and murdered four women. David John Birnie is such a danger to society that he should never be released from prison."

David Birnie was shaking on the bench when the sentence was pronounced, but he made a final bravado when he was driven to the prison van. The angry crowd demanding his blood, David Birnie laid hands on his lips and kissed them.

Judged sane enough to appear, Catherine Margaret Birnie admitted responsibility for the murders and was presented on 3 March 1987 to the Supreme Court of Perth. She was on the bench, holding hands with

An unprecedented case
in this isolated part of the world.

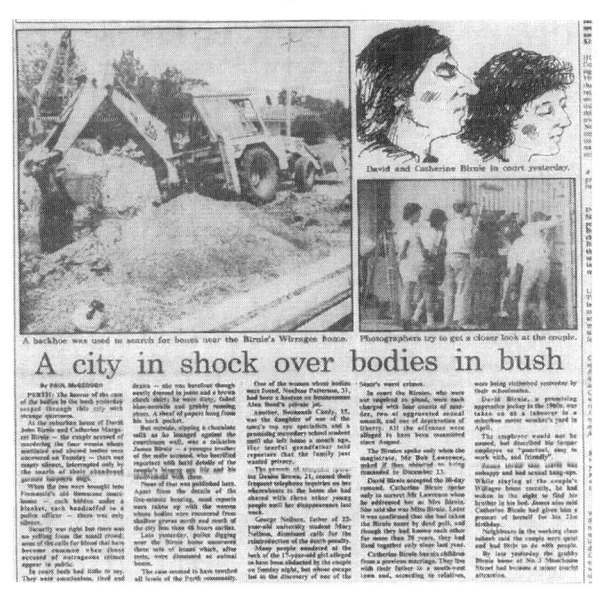

David Birnie, the man who had led her straight to hell. Throughout the day, they chatted quietly and smiled tenderly as the court was informed of the details of their 35-day murder orgies.

Sometimes she would stroke his arm. A court psychiatrist stated that Catherine was totally dependent on Birnie and was totally vulnerable to his bad influence. He said, "This is the worst case of emotional addiction I've seen in my career."

Justice Wallace was not hesitant to give the same sentence as that given to David Birnie. "In my opinion, you should never be released to find David Birnie. You should never be allowed to see him again."

In the following years, the Birnies often made headlines in local newspapers. In their first four years of incarceration, they exchanged 2,600 letters but were denied the right to marry, telephone or visit.

In 1990, David Birnie claimed that the denial of these rights imposed on them "a punishment beyond that prescribed by law". He told the media that he and Catherine were being physically and mentally tortured, and that refusing to let them have contact was an attempt to drive them to depression and suicide.

In 1992, the Perth Crime Squad granted David Birnie the rare privilege of seeing the outside world again as they drove him around Perth and its suburbs for five hours in the hope that he might confess to other murders he may have committed, in vain.

In 1993, David Birnie's personal computer was confiscated from his cell at the Casuarina prison protection unit when it was discovered that it contained pornographic material.

On 22 January 2000, Donald McLaughlan, the first husband of Catherine Birnie and father of her six children, died suddenly at the age of 59. Catherine Birnie submitted a request to the prison judge to attend her ex-husband's funeral, but this was refused.

Commenting on the refusal of the Department of Justice, the Premier of Western Australia, Richard Court, said: "As far as I am concerned, by the nature of their crimes, the Birnies have renounced forever this kind of privilege."

David was found dead in his cell at the Casuarina prison on 7 October 2005, 4:30 a.m. He was 54 years old. An investigation revealed that he had hung himself from a vent. Various factors led to his suicide: the withdrawal of antidepressants he had been prescribed had exacerbated his depression, he no longer had his computer, and was suspected of sexually assaulting another prisoner. Despite this, he was described by a former prison officer as a "model prisoner" who cared for injured animals. Once again, Catherine was not allowed to attend his funeral.

Catherine is still incarcerated in the Bandyup Women's Prison. Her parole applications are consistently denied. Opponents of her release claim that her harmless behavior behind bars (where she holds a librarian position) is misleading. They recall, for example, that ten years ago, she helped a vampire killer twenty years older than her, Jessica Stasinowsky, incarcerated in the same wing as her, to pass on words, and even a knife, to her lover Valerie, imprisoned in another wing.

In December 2006, Jessica Stasinowsky, 22, and Valerie Parashumti, 21, two lesbian *"vampyre"* goths, strangled with a chain and smashed the skull of 16-year-old Stacey Mitchell in a Lathlain home. They were arrested when police discovered the body of the teenager in a wheelie bin located in their shed.

The two women, still in love with each other (they knew each other only two months before the murder that had sent them to prison), had then benefited from the services of Catherine Birnie to maintain their flame.

Because of this incident, Birnie was transferred to another wing of the prison and since then her parole requests have never been taken seriously.

The Birnies' house located at 3 Moorhouse Street, in the suburbs of Willagee, although it has undergone several renovations, is still standing, and often the subject of visits from Australian lovers of macabre tourism. According to one of the developers who has been putting it on the market in recent years, "none of the former owners have ever complained about paranormal events."

Jessica Stasinowsky and Valerie Parashumti,
the vampire lesbian killers of Perth.

Michel Fourniret and Monique Olivier

Michel Fourniret was born on 4 April 1942 in Sedan, France. The son of an alcoholic metallurgist and a housewife, his acquaintances remember him as a quiet and intelligent child who loved chess and classical music. He later claimed to have been sexually assaulted in his childhood by his mother when he was 5 years old. His brother André would deny this claim during the investigation.

His brother and sister were older than him. An event of harmless appearance traumatized him when he was a child: he caught his big sister defecating in a bucket. He would later say: "For me, a woman does not defecate. It is degrading, it does not live up to the image of the Blessed Virgin."

As an adult, he took a series of subordinate jobs, including those of a forestry worker and a carpenter, after a short stint in Algeria as an airborne commando.

FOLIE À DEUX

He married for the first time in 1964 to a woman named Annette, with whom he had his first child. This did not prevent him from assaulting a minor, which sent him to prison. His wife divorced him, and he remarried a woman named Nicole, who gave him three children.

Until 1973, Michel Fourniret became accustomed to the courts. Voyeurism, inappropriate touching, violence, the motives were always the same. The court sentenced him more than ten years later for the rape of a dozen minors. His second wife also divorced him while he was serving a seven-year prison sentence.

Fourniret began to write to Monique Olivier via a small ad. In total, they would exchange more than 200 letters. He gradually told her about his fantasies of rape and murder of virgin girls; she replied that she would "help" him to realize these fantasies if he killed her husband. Why was she so eager to become an accomplice of these dark desires? Let us go back to the childhood of the woman who would later be called the "ogress".

Born on 31 October 1948 in Tours, Monique Olivier was the youngest of four children. Her father was a painter, her mother took care of the home. In this modest family of Nantes, the girl put an end to her studies and got small jobs as a secretary. Her health was fragile and shortly after her 20th birthday, she met her first husband, an amateur painter, with whom she would have two children in the early eighties.

But the romance went sour. Monique Olivier complained of mistreatment. Divorce occurred after a decade. She was a little over 30 years old, was hardly able to see her child again and lived a period of emotional instability. It was during this difficult period of her career that this woman came across a classified ad written by Michel Fourniret, and published in the magazine *Le Pèlerin*, a Catholic newspaper.

Fourniret was released on 22 October 1987. He moved in with his new girlfriend, who lived in Saint-Cyr-les-Colons, not far from Auxerre, the hunting ground of another famous serial killer, Émile Louis. A year later, a son was born from the union of the two lovebirds: Sélim. He played a crucial role in the events to come.

On 11 December 1987, Fourniret and Olivier drove separately towards Auxerre. When they saw Isabelle Laville, 17, who they had spotted a day or two earlier, walking home from school, Olivier stopped to ask the girl to join her in the car to give her directions, which Laville agreed to do. As she drove down the road, Olivier reached the spot where Fourniret was waiting quietly, standing beside his car, pretending that it had broken down. After Olivier, as planned, stopped to pick him up, he got into the car. Fourniret choked Laville with a piece of rope before Olivier put her to sleep with Rohypnol. The couple took the girl to their home in Saint-Cyr-les-Colons, where Fourniret raped and strangled her to death. They dumped Laville's body in a disused well at Bussy-en-Othe. Her remains were found in the well more than eighteen years later, on 11

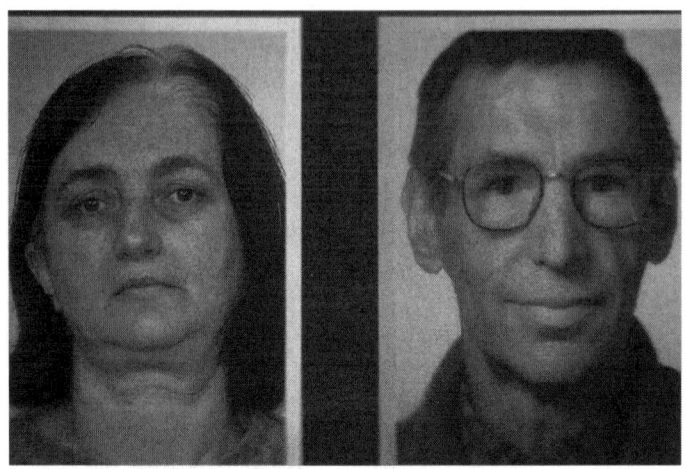

The Fourniret case has been making headlines
for decades in France.

The vehicle used by the ogre of the Ardennes.

July 2006. It should be noted that before the confession of Fourniret, the disappearance of Isabelle Laville had been attributed to Émile Louis.

At the prison of Fleury-Mérogis, Fourniret shared a cell with Jean-Pierre Hellegouarch, a former Action Direct member serving a sentence for robbery. Presumably unaware of the honor code that forbids a bank robber from having any kind of positive interaction with a rapist, especially a pedophile, Hellegouarch explained to Fourniret that he knew the location of a treasure buried in a grave at a cemetery in Fontenay-en-Parisis, in the Val-d'Oise. Once out, Fourniret offered to recover the treasure with the help of the robber's companion, a woman named Farida Hammiche. After Fourniret and Hammiche managed to recover the loot, consisting of gold bars and coins, Hammiche gave Fourniret a share of 500,000 francs to help her bring the loot back to her apartment in Vitry-sur-Seine. On 12 April, in order to steal Hammiche's share, Fourniret and Olivier lured the young woman out of her home. They took her to Clairefontaine-en-Yvelines, where they strangled her and buried her in a quarry. The couple then broke into Hammiche's house and stole the loot. They used the money to buy a manor called Château du Sautou, in Donchery, in the Ardennes. Hammiche's body was never found. When he was arrested years later, Michel Fourniret only commented with the laconic phrase: "There was no sexual aspect to this crime, it was only a transfer of ownership."

On 3 August, the couple drove to a supermarket in Châlons-sur-Marne (today Châlons-en-Champagne) and met Fabienne Leroy, 20 years old, in the parking lot. Olivier, pregnant, faked being sick and the duo asked Leroy to join them in their car and give them directions to a doctor. Once the girl was on board, the couple drove to a forest near the military camp of Mourmelon-le-Grand. Fourniret ordered Olivier to inspect Leroy's hymen to see if it was still intact, but she refused. After raping her, the ex-con shot her in the chest. Her body was later found in the woods.

In January 1989, Fourniret crossed the path of Jeanne-Marie Desramault, 22 years old, on a train to Charleville-Mézières. The two conversed before arriving at Charleville, where Desramault was staying in a convent. Desramault again met Fourniret and Olivier at the station on March 18, and the couple invited her to come to their home in Floing – a proposal she accepted without batting an eyelid – Fourniret promising that he would take her home afterwards. After arriving in Floing, Fourniret asked Desramault if she was a virgin. She answered no, and that she had a boyfriend. Enraged, he attacked her. She defended herself as he tried to rape her, and while she tried to escape, the couple gagged her with adhesive tape before Fourniret strangled her. Fourniret and Olivier then went to Donchery and buried the body of Desramault in the garden of the castle of Sautou.

Let's go back a little bit to what was going on in this famous castle. According to some testimonies, Fourniret had set up a torture room in the attic for his criminal and libertine activities. William M., one of

Monique Olivier's children from her previous marriage, later told reporters:

"What really stuck out to me when I was there was the fact that we were limited in our movements by Fourniret. I never went inside," he added, noting that the serial killer and his accomplice were actually living "clustered" with the children in a little adjacent home, not in the castle itself. "The access was blocked, he had formally forbidden me from going inside. The whole interior of the castle was closed for 'work', so they said." And it was especially the "top floor" of the building to which Michel Fourniret forbade access. "To dissuade us from entering, Fourniret had given the excuse that there was a hornet invasion on the top floor. A deadly danger, he claimed... In retrospect, when we know what was found in the woods surrounding the park, we dare not imagine what he was doing up there," continued Olivier's son. "In hindsight, I came to realize what was probably inside the castle.... An above-ground cemetery," said William M., concluding: "It was a playroom, if you know what I mean... who knows what would have happened to me if I had ever discovered its secret?" Michel Fourniret, in a letter to his son Sélim in January 2016, mentioned a secret staircase that was very inconspicuous. "In the shadows, the Devil is laying out his plans".

Fourniret and Olivier married in July 1989. On the afternoon of 20 December, they crossed the Franco-Belgian border by car to Saint-Servais, Namur, with their one-year-old son. Fourniret found Élisabeth Brichet, 12 years old, while she was walking to a friend's house, and waited for her outside until she took the short road that led to her home just before 7:00pm. He asked her to give him the address of a doctor for his son. She agreed, and the couple returned to Floing with her. When Fourniret undressed the girl, he found that she was having her period, so he asked Olivier to clean her genitals. The next day, the couple took Brichet to the castle, where Fourniret strangled her after a failed attempt to suffocate her with a plastic bag. Her body was buried in the garden of the castle, near that of Jeanne-Marie Desramault.

The little Brichet girl was the subject of several reports after her disappearance by people who said they had seen her in Belgium and abroad, and a number of people were suspected by the police to have kidnapped her, including another serial killer, Marc Dutroux. After the arrest of Dutroux in 1996, Brichet's mother, Marie-Noëlle Bouzet, participated in the organization of the "White March" in honor of the missing and murdered children in Belgium. The remains of Brichet and Desramault were exhumed from the garden of the Château du Sautou on 3 July 2004, after Fourniret and Olivier confessed to the murders.

The body of Joanna Parrish, a 20-year-old British teacher at the Jacques-Amyot high school in Auxerre, was found on 17 May 1990 in a river in Moneteau (Yonne) after being raped, beaten and strangled. Fourniret confessed to killing her in February 2018.

The last known murder committed by Fourniret with the help of Olivier took place on 21 November 1990 near Nantes. The couple drove to a shopping center in Rezé after leaving the court in Nantes, where they had been convicted of burglary. They spotted Natacha Danais, a 13-year-old girl, walking in the parking lot towards her home after being sent to fetch her mother's forgotten bag. The couple lured Danais into their van, asking for directions. After driving her to an isolated area near the coast, Fourniret stabbed Danais twice in the chest with a screwdriver and strangled her before leaving her body on the beach. The post-mortem examination suggested that the girl's body had been raped after the murder. An individual close to the ETA terrorist organization would be unjustly accused of this murder and later committed suicide in prison.

The Fourniret family moved to Sart-Custinne, Gedinne, Belgium in the early 1990s. Fourniret admitted to committing two other murders in France between 2000 and 2001, after a nine-and-a-half-year lull. On 16 May 2000, he crossed the Franco-Belgian border alone to Charleville-Mézières and lured 18-year-old Céline Saison into his van late in the afternoon. On the way to Belgium, he raped her before strangling her with a rope and dumping her body in a forest in Sugny, Vresse-sur-Semois. The remains of Saison were discovered by mushroom foragers on 22 July 2000.

In March 2002, it was the turn of Mananya Thumpong, a 13-year-old daughter of Thai origin, to disappear in Sedan. Her bones were found a year later, 30 kilometers away.

One of the most famous victims of Michel Fourniret was probably his last. On January 9, 2003, Estelle Mouzin, a 9-year-old girl born on June 29, 1993, disappeared on the way back from the school in Guermantes, while she was returning to her mother's home, who was divorcing from her father, Éric Mouzin, who lived about 60 kilometers away in Vésinet, with their eldest son, Arthur. Her mother, returning from work, reported her disappearance at the local police station in Lagny-sur-Marne at 7:30pm. After his arrest, Michel Fourniret would tell the investigators who suspected him of this kidnapping that the disappearance of the girl was "a subject to dig". Monique Olivier would affirm in 2020, through a lawyer, that her ex-husband had kidnapped Estelle on January 9, 2003, and that he had taken her to Ville-sur-Lumes, in the Ardennes, and that "he had raped and strangled her." Partial DNA traces of Estelle Mouzin were later found on a mattress in the old house of Fourniret's sister. Estelle's body would never be found.

There are several ways to explain the longevity of the criminal career of Michel Fourniret, who was well-known by the police for his subsequent convictions.

First, none of the abductions were considered part of a series. The places of the disappearances were sometimes distant, and Fourniret himself made sure to "hunt" his prey on the hunting grounds of other serial killers: Émile Louis, Pierre Chanal, Marc Dutroux... And above all, the Ardennes ogre used the pregnancy of his wife, then their baby, to reduce the mistrust of his potential victims. It was easy for him to get them into his car before immobilizing them and then transporting them to another area, away from the site of the abduction.

It would be easy to think that these schemes were the fruit of a highly intelligent and manipulative individual. However, those who have dealt with Michel Fourniret remember a small individual (1m62), intellectually mediocre, meek and very arrogant. He himself boasted of being a philosophy enthusiast and presented himself to expert psychiatrists as "an evil being devoid of all human feeling", but it seems that the brains of the Fourniret couple was indeed Monique Olivier, whose IQ far exceeded that of her partner.

Obsessed with the idea of stealing his victims' virginity, Fourniret limited his choice of victims to children and girls, whom he called MSP ("Membranes sur pattes"/"Two-legged membranes"). But sex was not the only driving factor. Greedy, he took the risk of becoming the target of a contract on behalf of a gang of bank robbers, furious that a rapist had stolen their money so easily. During his criminal career, he also made many mistakes, giving his real name to future victims, and always using the same vehicle to catch his prey. As is often the case in many serial murder cases, he didn't owe his arrest to the admirable investigative work of a handful of super investigators, but to his own clumsiness and the many clues he had left in his wake.

It was during an umpteenth attempt of abduction, on June 26, 2003, near Namur in Belgium, that the ogre of the Ardennes committed the mistake that would send

FOLIE À DEUX

Michel Fourniret bought a manor with the money
he had stolen from bankrobbers.

him to end his days in a maximum-security prison. Fourniret abducted 13-year-old Marie-Ascension on her way to a local shop. As with his other crimes, he used the same ruse, telling the girl that he was looking for a doctor. The girl showed him the direction but refused to get into the vehicle. Fourniret took an indignant air and with a stern look, he said to her: "It is not nice not to trust people!" This phrase and the tone he used convinced Marie-Ascension, who finally got on board. He started the car, passed by her school, and accelerated. On the way, Fourniret stopped in a parking lot, tied up the girl, moved her to the back of the van and then started to drive again. While the vehicle stopped at a crossroads about ten kilometers from the place of abduction, Marie-Ascension managed to open the back door and escape. She was taken care of by a motorist. As she saw the vehicle of Fourniret who had turned back, probably to try to find her, the driver noted the license plate of the C25 pickup, which allowed for the arrest of the 61-year-old serial killer at his home. A year later, the investigation proved Monique Olivier's involvement in the murders, and she was arrested as well.

The trial opened on 27 March 2008 at the assizes court of Charleville-Mézières. The accused decided to make a circus of the court, refusing to speak at the hearings and holding up a sign that read, "If the public is allowed inside the courtroom, I will shut my mouth." The prosecution tried to prove that Monique Olivier, far from being a simple submissive follower, was the "bloody muse" of the ogre. Both were sentenced to life in prison.

FOLIE À DEUX

Later, Michel Fourniret was transferred to Ensisheim prison, where he joined the local crime celebrities who were imprisoned there: Guy Georges, Émile Louis and Francis Heaulme. Monique Olivier was transferred to Rennes prison and the divorce between the two spouses was pronounced on 2 July 2010. She returned to court in 2023 for three more murders. In 2024, she was heard for yet another cold case, concerning the disappearance of Lydie Logé, 29 years old, in 1993.

On 10 May 2021, Michel Fourniret died of respiratory failure at the Pitié-Salpêtrière hospital in Paris. No one in his family claimed his remains, and he was buried in the square of the indigents of the cemetery of Thiais, also called "garden of fraternity". I don't know if it's a real sense of brotherhood that made me do this, but one week after his burial, with no real indication of where he was buried, I went to Thiais and walked through the five divisions of this famous "garden", which houses the remains of several thousand homeless people and individuals without family, and where they are buried for about five years until their remains are excavated and stored elsewhere. It is customary, even if these tombs are anonymous, to put on the gravestones a plaque indicating the date of death of the deceased, with their initials. The product used to glue this plaque was, according to my experience, not yet dry, and it would give easily under the pressure of a well-placed screwdriver. I saw a slab that seemed to have been laid recently, but there was no plaque on it. A year later, I returned to the scene, to be sure that it was indeed the tomb of the ogre. Strangely enough, this tomb still had no plaque, as if the cemetery administration wanted to preserve its anonymity at-all costs. Aside from the handful of people present at the burial, I think I'm one of the only people who knows the exact location of the grave of one of France's most famous serial killers.

In 2026, as required by law, his skeleton will be exhumed, his bones and skull will be placed in a wooden box called "reliquary", and this box, designated only by a number, will be piled among thousands of others about a hundred meters away, in a large underground complex with the appearance of a bunker, designated as an "ossuary" by the municipality. The funeral bureaucracy will then have definitively annihilated all traces of the presence on Earth of Michel Fourniret.

Charles Starkweather and Caril Fugate

In 1958, 19-year-old Charles Starkweather was an angry boy. Angry because he was not allowed to marry his girlfriend. Angry because he was broke. Angry because he felt he was trapped in remote Nebraska, where everyone thought he was a loser.

This rage turned into one of the most romanticized crime sprees of the 20th century. A whole bunch of films, songs and fictional characters were based on the duo he formed with Caril Fugate. Together, these two rockabilly teenagers embarked on a murderous madness that horrified the country.

It was a country that was undergoing major cultural changes. New symbols of rebellion had emerged: Elvis Presley, James Dean and rock 'n roll culture had caught a new generation that challenged the world of the 1950s. But this world so ordered, praising family values which had been until then undisputed - was it ready for a wild, blood-thirsty teenage couple?

Charlie Starkweather was born to a poor family in Lincoln, Nebraska on November 24, 1938. He was the third of seven children born to Guy and Helen Starkweather. Despite the precarious circumstances in which the family lived, the Starkweather children never suffered long periods without food or shelter. They were poor, but that did not prevent little Charlie from having a decent childhood and good family memories. Their neighbors considered the Starkweather children to be well behaved, and they were happy.

Guy was a carpenter by profession, but he would have preferred to make a career in an office. He did not have the physical stamina necessary for this job and suffered from a bad back. Helen, a small woman with red frizzy hair, was often described as strong and kind. She worked as a waitress to make ends meet.

While Charlie had nothing but good things to say about his family, his school experiences were traumatic. The sense of security he felt in his home environment evaporated in the classroom. The children mocked his slight stutter and teased him about his bowlegs. Even though Charlie was of average intelligence, he was considered to have learning difficulties. In addition, he was hampered by his severe myopia. He could not even read the larger letters on the board.

One of the few subjects he excelled at was sports. He was strong and particularly agile for his age. His gymnastics skills were his only legitimate source of pride. The other side of the coin was that he used those same physical abilities to continually fight with the other boys in school. He quickly gained a reputation as Lincoln's most brawler student.

In college, he met Bob Von Busch, who, after Charlie had fought with him, became one of his closest friends. Bob said of Charlie, "He could be the nicest person you've ever met. He would do anything for you if he liked you. He was also very funny. It was all a joke to him. But he had another darker side. He could be mean and cruel. If he saw a poor fellow on the street who was taller than him, more handsome or better dressed, he would do anything to make him look down."

Both boys were James Dean fanatics; they had seen all his films. Charlie tried to imitate Dean's manners, clothes and hairstyle, wearing the same tight jeans and cowboy boots. But Charlie didn't have much of James Dean, not his beauty, or his intelligence, or his talent. He was just a very imperfect imitation. What was authentic about Charlie, however, was the sense of rebellion that Dean embodied on screen.

Bob Von Busch began dating Barbara Fugate in 1956. Charlie liked Barbara's younger sister, Caril, who had just turned 13. The four teenagers were together regularly, despite Caril's youth.

Caril was a pretty girl with dark brown hair and a bright smile. She too had a rebellious spirit and temperament. Charlie treated her like a goddess. And because of his youth, she thought he was cool and only saw the good in him. She was impressed by his car, tenacity, appearance and - despite his poverty - how he could give her almost everything she wanted... Charlie said that Caril meant more to him than anything before. Caril almost made him stop hating the whole world. She made him feel like he was worth something, in the end.

Charlie left school at the age of sixteen to load and unload trucks at the Western Newspaper Union warehouse. His boss had a low opinion of him: "Sometimes you had to tell him something two or three times in a row. Of all the employees in the warehouse, he was by far the stupidest."

The warehouse was located near the school that Caril attended, and he saw her every day. He taught her to drive, even though she was too young to get a license. One day, Caril had a minor accident with her lover's speedster. Charlie's father was partly the owner of the car and had to pay for the damage done to the other vehicle, an event that caused a huge dispute between father and son. They clashed, and Charlie was forced to find another place to sleep.

Charlie moved into a guest room in the house of his friend Bob and Barbara Fugate, who had just married him. Now that the relationship with his parents was very tense, Caril became the center of Charlie's life. He began to tell people that he and Caril would soon be married, then he told his friends that Caril was pregnant with his child - a lie that turned against him when Caril's parents heard it.

Charlie quit his job at the paper mill and started working as a garbage collector. It wasn't much better, but he took the job to be available when she left school. The salary was only $42 a week - not enough to support himself, let alone Caril.

Charlie began to feel trapped in a life of poverty. With his limited intellect, the only way out he could think of was to do something extremely illegal and lucrative - like rob a bank. Every day on his way, when he was picking up trash on the other side of town, where Lincoln's middle and upper classes lived, he saw everything that he was excluded from... While lifting heavy stinking bags of garbage for a wretched wage, Starkweather realized that, for him, there was only one way to fight against the class system that he so despised, even if he had no real political conscience: only the dead are all at the same level.

Little by little, Charlie became convinced that he would have to make a career in crime to get the money and respect he so badly craved. One day he wanted to buy a stuffed dog for Caril at a gas station and realized that he didn't even have enough money for it. Worse, the gas station attendant refused to let him buy the stuffed animal on credit. Charlie was convinced: he had to make them all pay.

The temperatures were freezing and the winds from Nebraska swept mercilessly on that first day of December 1957. It was almost 3 o'clock in the morning. It was time to start making them understand what he was capable of.

FOLIE À DEUX

Charlie grabbed a 12-gauge rifle he had stolen from Bob Von Busch's cousin and went to the gas station that had refused him credit.

Robert Colvert, the 21-year-old man who had humiliated Charlie the day before, was alone that day. He was a small, thin man who was about to become a father.

Colvert was working on a carburetor when Charlie entered the gas station. He sold him a pack of Camels and his client left without saying anything. A few minutes later, Charlie turned around and returned to the gas station. Colvert was still behind the counter. This time, Charlie bought a pack of gum, got in his car and drove away.

He pulled over and put on a disguise: a bandana tied around his face and a hunter's cap to cover his red hair. Then Charlie returned to the gas station with the loaded gun and a canvas bag to put his loot in.

At this point, Colvert was working on a car again and didn't even notice someone was there until he felt the tip of a gun against his back. Charlie took Colvert to the counter and made him open the cash drawer.

The robber took some money and put it in the canvas bag. *"Open the safe!"* he yelled, but Colvert did not have the combination; only the boss knew it. Charlie accepted this explanation and decided to settle for the hundred dollars that were in the cash drawer.

The robber ordered Colvert to take a ride with him and had his hostage lead them to the house of "Bloody Mary". Bloody Mary was a crazy old woman who did not hesitate to use her shotgun on anyone who entered her property.

Charlie pulled Colvert out of the car. Later, Charlie claimed that Colvert tried to grab his weapon and he had to shoot him to defend himself. However, when Colvert tried to get on his hands and knees, Charlie shot him once more in the skull.

The newspapers made this murder and theft a major news event, as crimes of this magnitude were rare in the region. Starkweather took the precaution of painting his car a different color, but this did not prevent him from exhibiting suspicious behavior afterwards. Most of the loot from the gas station was coins, which Charlie used to buy clothes. Fortunately for him, the authorities thought that the robbery and murder had been committed by a passing stranger.

The murder gave Starkweather a sense of euphoria and peace. He had money. He had a girlfriend. He had killed, with no consequences for himself. It gave him a tremendous sense of power. He felt beyond the reach of men's laws; it was as if he were invisible, he could do whatever he wanted, take whatever he wanted.

The day after the crime, Charlie admitted to Caril that he had robbed the gas station, but that someone else had shot Colvert. *"I was not fooled,"* she said later.

The murder created a bond between them that sealed their fate.

When the initial euphoria dissipated, Charlie found himself faced with a grim reality: he had been fired from his job as a garbage man; his landlord had evicted him because he was behind on his rent; his family and Caril's were completely hostile to their relationship. Caril had gained some weight, and her family was sure she was pregnant. The young killer was desperate.

On a Tuesday afternoon, January 21, 1958, Starkweather went to the slum that Caril and her family called their home. The building and courtyard were littered with waste and unused construction materials. Charlie took the 22-gauge gun he had borrowed and some ammunition, went to the back door and knocked. Caril's mother, Velda Bartlett, came to greet him.

What happened next is impossible to confirm. This story is based on Starkweather's memories after the fact. He claimed that he had brought the gun and ammunition in hopes of going hunting with Caril's father-in-law, Marion Bartlett, to try and improve their relationship. He had also brought with him two carpets for Velda.

According to Charlie, Velda and Marion were both in the house. Their two-and-a-half-year-old child, Betty Jean, was crying. Velda told Charlie that they didn't want him to see Caril anymore.

Charles Starkweather, the poor man's James Dean, did not need to make much effort to win the favor of Caril Fugate.

FOLIE À DEUX

A strong dispute ensued, and Velda allegedly hit Charlie several times. He claimed to have left the house without the gun and had been riding for a while before returning to get his weapon. When he came back, Marion literally kicked him out.

Starkweather went to a phone booth, called Marion Bartlett's place of work and told them that he was sick and would not be at work for a few days. Then he went back to Caril's and waited for her outside the house. When Charlie told Caril what had happened with her parents, she entered the house and quarreled with her mother. Starkweather followed her into the house.

He claimed that Velda started hitting him again, yelling that he had got Caril pregnant. He hit Velda "in defense" and they struggled for a few minutes before Charlie could get his hands on his gun. At that moment, Marion Bartlett entered the room, allegedly with a hammer in his hand, and Starkweather shot him in the head. Then, Charlie claimed that Velda charged him with a huge knife. Starkweather shot her in the face. As if that wasn't enough, he smashed her skull with the butt of his rifle when she tried to get up and reach for her baby. Then Charlie stabbed little Betty Jean.

Starkweather stated: "I picked up the knife that the old woman had in her hands... I started walking into the room... and the little girl kept screaming, and I told her to shut up, and I started walking again, and I just turned around and threw the kitchen knife at her... they said that the knife had hit her in the throat, but

I'm sure it hit her in the chest... I went into the room. Mr. Bartlett was still moving, so I tried to stab him in the throat, but the knife wouldn't go in, so I pressed my palm on the handle and it went in like butter."

The reaction and role of Caril in this butchery have never been determined very clearly. Since the only two living witnesses were Charlie and Caril, the truth might never be known. Caril claimed that she had broken up with Charlie before these tragic events and was terrified while he attacked her family. But what happened after her family was killed is beyond belief.

Velda's body was dragged into the old outbuilding and pushed into the toilet. Her baby was placed in a box used for garbage and taken to the outside toilet. Marion Bartlett was dragged to the chicken coop.

Once they were done with this, Caril and Charlie cleaned up the blood and mess inside and spent the rest of the evening drinking Pepsi and eating chips. They stayed in the house, a few meters from the rotting corpses of Caril's family, for almost a week, buying milk and bread on credit from the dairy every day. Charlie would sometimes go to the grocery store to buy some other essentials.

In the days following the murders, a number of visitors came to the house but did not go beyond the threshold. Caril had a sign on the front door that said, "Go away, everybody is sick with the flu."

FOLIE À DEUX

One day, Marion Bartlett's boss came knocking on the door to see how sick he was, but Caril went out and told him that her father was still very ill and lying down. Then Caril's sister, Barbara Von Busch, and her husband came to visit them, but Caril discouraged both of them with this flu story. However, they both suspected something was wrong and later Bob Von Busch returned with his brother to investigate. This time the story had changed. In tears, Caril told them they had to go away. "Please don't try to get in. Mom's life depends on it!" The von Busch brothers then went to the police station.

Later, the police arrived, and Caril told them that her entire family had the flu. When an agent asked her why her brother-in-law was so worried, Caril told them that Bob Von Busch was always too worried about them. As Caril seemed sincere and credible, and she did not seem in danger, they left without searching the property. Later, the Von Buschs were told that there was no reason to be alarmed.

Bob and Barbara sent one of Caril's close friends to visit her, and this time she gave him a third version of the story. Caril said to his friend in a low voice, "A guy is over there with Chuck. He's got a machine gun. I think they're going to rob a bank." The friend did not tell the Von Busches, but told her father, who called the police the next day.

Caril's grandmother, Pansy, came to her daughter's house. Caril seemed to know that her grandmother was not going to buy this flu story, so she uttered a vague threat: "Go home, Grandma. Oh, Grandma, go! Mom will be in danger if you don't."

Pansy got angry, "If you don't open that door right now, I'm going to get a search warrant."

Caril refused to let her in, and Pansy turned and left. Eventually, the police, at Pansy's insistence, went to look inside the house, even though she had no warrant. There was no one inside. Officers found that there did not appear to be any signs of violence inside the house.

Later that day, Bob Von Busch demanded that the police conduct a thorough search of the property, but they refused. Meanwhile, Guy Starkweather had tried to get the police to go and interrogate his son, but they were unsuccessful.

Bob Von Busch and his brother went to the Bartletts' house and searched the property from top to bottom. The inspection of the outside toilet and the chicken coop confirmed their worst fears. This time, the police paid some attention to them.

Charlie Starkweather and Caril Fugate were immediately placed on the most country's most wanted list, but what the police didn't know was that this only was the second act of this tragedy.

Once Starkweather and Caril realized they had better leave town, they understood that Charlie's car was not going to take them very far. The tires were flat, and it became urgent to find a garage. He knew he could find temporary shelter at a friend of his family, August Meyer. Meyer was an old bachelor who had known Charlie since he was a kid. He had a farm about 20 miles from Lincoln, where Charlie would go hunting sometimes. On January 27, the couple engaged on the dirt track leading to Meyer's farm, but the vehicle immediately got stuck.

It's difficult to determine exactly what happened next, because the versions given by Caril and Charlie were very contradictory, but what is certain is that Charlie shot August Meyer in the head. As in the other murders, Charlie unconvincingly claimed that he had acted in self-defense. According to Charlie, Meyer tried to shoot him, and the gun jammed, so Charlie fired back. Then he had wounded Meyer's dog as it ran through the snowy meadow.

Charlie dragged his old friend's body into a building and hid it under a blanket. Then he and Caril went into Meyer's house, stole his money and weapons, ate his food and fell asleep peacefully.

The next day, a neighbor helped them to get their vehicle out, and they went to the farm by another road. When Charlie checked his friend's body, he was frightened by the fact that the blanket had mysteriously disappeared during the night. Fearing they had been discovered, Charlie and Caril drove their car down the same path in which they had become stuck. Unsurprisingly, the couple, who could not be described as particularly clever, found themselves trapped once more. Taking only their weapons, they left the old Ford where it was.

Hiding their shotguns, they were picked up on the road by Robert Jensen, 17, and Carol King, 16. After a few minutes, Charlie pointed his gun at Jensen's neck and asked him for money. He forced the driver back to Meyer's farm and took the couple down into an abandoned cellar.

There he fired six bullets into Jensen's head. Carol King, his girlfriend, received a single bullet in the head. Her body was found half naked, her jeans and panties lowered around her ankles. She had been stabbed repeatedly in the abdomen and pubis, but there was no trace of semen in or around her vagina.

All the while, Caril was sitting in the car. Charlie later attributed the mutilation of King's body to Caril, who was supposedly angry at the dead girl for "flirting" with her boyfriend. At another time, Charlie claimed that Caril had also killed the hostage while he was in another location.

The two teenagers' bodies were left in the cellar while Charlie and Caril left in Jensen's car. Once again, the couple were victims of their own stupidity. Instead of trying to leave the state as quickly as possible, they returned to Lincoln, where everyone knew them, and dozens of police officers were looking for them.

As if that wasn't enough, they passed by the Bartletts' house to see if the bodies of Caril's parents had been discovered. They got their answer when they saw all the police cars parked around the property. Eventually, they went to the nice neighborhoods of the city and fell asleep in their stolen car.

FOLIE À DEUX

The next day, on 28 January 1958, Starkweather's car was spotted, stuck near the Meyer farm. Shortly afterwards, the bodies of the owner and the two teenagers were found. A massive manhunt was organized, but there were still more murders to come.

Despite his poverty, Charlie was very familiar with the upscale neighborhoods, because of his former job as a garbage man. He decided to target the large house of C. Lauer Ward, 47, a close friend of the governor, chairman of the companies Capital Bridge and Capital Steel.

That morning, Clara Ward, the chairman's wife, and Lillian Fencl, their fifty-one-year-old hearing-impaired maid, were at home, as was their golden retriever Queenie, and their little poodle, Suzy.

When Lillian Fencl opened the door, Charlie pointed his gun at her. Caril stayed in the car. He ordered Lillian to lock Queenie in the basement. Realizing that the maid had a hearing problem, he wrote notes to her to make himself understood and ordered her to continue preparing breakfast for Mrs. Ward.

When Clara Ward entered the kitchen, Charlie assured her that he would not harm her. Clara remained calm and agreed to cooperate. Charlie brought Caril to the house where Mrs. Ward had made him coffee, and Caril went into the library and fell asleep.

Charlie ordered Clara Ward to make pancakes for him and serve them in the library. When everything was ready, he changed his mind and had waffles made instead. Despite this, Mrs. Ward kept her composure and was always kind to Charlie. He was proud of himself: he, the former garbage man, finding himself in the slippers of one of Lincoln's richest residents and giving orders to his wife.

At about 1 pm, Clara Ward asked for permission to go upstairs and change shoes. After a few minutes, Charlie went upstairs to see what was keeping her. He claimed she had a .22-caliber pistol, which she fired and dropped. Charlie threw a knife in her back. He then stabbed her repeatedly in the neck and chest.

As he dragged Clara's body into the room, Suzy started barking at him. He broke its neck with a stick.

After killing Clara Ward, Starkweather called his father and asked him to tell Bob Von Busch that he was going to kill him for trying to stop her from seeing Caril. Later, the couple loaded food into Ward's 1956 black Packard convertible to continue their carnage elsewhere. They ransacked the house, taking everything that seemed precious to them.

Around 5:30 p.m., the local newspaper from Lincoln was delivered to the front door and Charlie was delighted: "Hey, Caril, look! We are famous! We're front-page news." He had finally reached glory, taking great pride in being able to read his name spread on the headlines.

FOLIE À DEUX

Robert Colvert, 21
Gas station attendant.

Velda Bartlett, 36
Marion Bartlett, 58
Caril's mother &
stepfather.

Betty Jean, 2
Caril's baby
half-sister.

August Meyer, 70
Farmer & friend
of Charlie
Starkweather.

Carol King, 16
High school
student.

Robert Jensen, 17
High school
student.

Clara Ward, 46
Housewife.

C. Lauer Ward, 48
Businessman

Lillian Fencl, 51
Maid.

Merle Collison, 37
Salesman

The eleven victims
of Starkweather and Fugate.

The black convertible Packard that was stolen by the lovers
during their murder spree.

Half an hour later, C. Lauer Ward returned from work and found himself with the barrel of Starkweather's gun pointed at him. After a short fight, Charlie took over and eventually shot him down. Then he went after Lillian Fencl. Caril and Charlie tied her to a bed and stabbed her to death. Charlie claimed that it was Caril who killed the maid, while Caril claimed that it was Charlie who had done it. Oddly, this time, Charlie did not try to justify the murder by claiming that the maid had attacked him.

The next day, Ward's cousin and partner noticed he was missing from work and called home all morning. Then, at about noon, he went to his house. He found the bodies of Ward, his wife, and the maid. Downstairs, Queenie was barking furiously and upstairs, Suzy was curled up under the bed, its neck broken.

Governor Anderson was immediately informed of the savage attack on his friend. Shortly after, he called the National Guard, and they quickly patrolled the streets of the city with jeeps armed with machine guns. Worried parents rushed into schools and brought their children home. The city was in shock.

The FBI opened an investigation. A $1,000 reward for any information leading to the arrest of the suspects was offered by the mayor. Planes were flying over the area to help locate the Ward's black Packard convertible.

And where do you think these crime geniuses went first? To Caril's parents, of course! However, seeing that there was a car in the driveway and that the house was lit up, they had the good sense not to stop there. It was time for them to head west, towards Washington State.

They drove all night and crossed Wyoming the next morning, on January 29, 1958. On two occasions, they were reported to the police as acting in a suspicious manner, but to no avail. On the way, they looked for another car to steal and eventually ran into Merle Collison, a traveling shoe salesman from Montana, who was sleeping in his Buick parked along the highway.

Charlie woke the salesman to tell him they were exchanging cars, but the shoe salesman was too slow to react, and Charlie shot him in the head several times. Once again, Charlie later reported that it was Caril who had killed him.

With the corpse of Collison sitting in the front passenger seat and Caril in the back, Starkweather started the car but couldn't figure out how to release the brake. A few minutes later, a young motorist stopped to help the couple, thinking they were having car problems.

"Hands off!" said Charlie, pointing the gun at him. "Help me to release the brake or I will kill you."

When the good Samaritan saw the dead man in the passenger seat, he realized that he had to grab Starkweather's gun if he wanted to stay alive. While they were struggling, seeing the scene, William Romer, a deputy sheriff of Wyoming, stopped at their level.

Immediately, Caril jumped from the back seat and ran to Romer. "Take me to the police!" she exclaimed.

"Well, I'm a deputy sheriff," he replied.

"He killed a man," she said, crying and pointing to the car.

At that time, Charlie had taken refuge behind the wheel of the Packard and was speeding towards the city of Douglas. Romer asked his colleagues to set up a roadblock and went after him. Douglas police chief Robert Ainslie, who was in his car with County Sheriff Earl Heflin, received the call from Romer.

When the Packard convertible drove pass them on the road leading to Douglas, the two men set out after it, with Heflin shooting the car through his window. Suddenly, Starkweather stopped abruptly in the middle of the highway.

The two experienced policemen stopped behind the vehicle and waited for Starkweather to come out. They ordered Charlie to raise his hands, but he refused to comply, so Ainslee shot at the ground near his feet. This time, Ainslie ordered him to lie down on the ground, but instead, Charlie slipped his hand behind his pants. Thinking that Charlie was looking for a gun in his back pocket, Ainslie shot near his feet again. At this point, Charlie decided to lie down as he was ordered. He let the officers put the handcuffs on him, a quiet end for a young man who had just killed 11 people.

FOLIE À DEUX

From a media point of view, Starkweather was the first teenage killer to make headlines, long before the Columbine murders. From a legal point of view, his options were not looking great. He could either go to the gas chamber in Wyoming for the murder of Merle Collison or he could end up on the electric chair in Nebraska for his many other murders there. He chose Nebraska and he and Caril were extradited there in late January 1958. What he didn't know, and that nobody had thought to tell him, was that if he had stayed in Wyoming, he would probably have been sentenced to life, the governor of Wyoming being an opponent of the death penalty.

Caril, meanwhile, maintained that she had been a hostage throughout this ordeal and had followed Charlie because she feared he would kill the rest of her family if she did not. The only problem with this story was that she admitted to being present for all the murders in Nebraska, which included her parents and half-sister.

Charlie and Caril were both charged with murder, and robbery. As both were judged as adults, the two faced the prospect of the electric chair. The prosecution, represented by prosecutor Elmer Scheele, chose to focus on the murder of Robert Jensen to try them, as it had the best potential to shock and outrage the jury.

Charlie's trial began on 5 May 1958. He did nothing to improve his situation. He claimed to be completely sane while his lawyers desperately tried to put together a defense based on psychiatric irresponsibility. But for

Charlie, being considered insane was much worse than being a cold-blooded murderer.

T. Clement Gaughan and William F. Matschullat were appointed by the court to carry out the difficult task of defending Charlie. They had to prove that Starkweather was completely crazy, while the prosecutor had a relatively easy task: proving that Charlie was sane when he had killed Jensen.

Initially, Charlie had told investigators that Caril had nothing to do with the crimes. His first words on the subject when he was taken to a Wyoming prison were, *"Don't be hard on her. She didn't do anything."*

The passing of time and the prospect of being burned alive on an electric chair becoming more and more palpable, Charlie realized that Caril was trying to pass herself off as a reluctant hostage instead of his girlfriend, and he began to implicate her in the crimes. He suggested that she was responsible for many of the murders and all the knife mutilations.

"She could have escaped at any time," said Starkweather. "I've left her alone many times. Sometimes when I went to get burgers, she was sitting in the car with all the guns. Nothing would have stopped her from running away."

One of the defense lawyers, Clement Gaughan, made a very moving plea: "This boy is a product of our society. The society that spawned this individual is looking for a scapegoat. Caril Fugate must receive the same punishment as this boy, but I can tell you that she will never be sentenced to death. His life, my life, were almost similar until our nineteenth birthday. I say it without shame. As a teenager, I hated everyone. Society treated me exactly the way it treated Charles Starkweather, but God gave me better parents."

The jury rendered its decision in less than twenty-four hours: Starkweather was found guilty of both counts of first-degree murder. The men and women of the jury specifically requested that he be sentenced to death. Their request was granted on 25 June 1959.

At the Caril trial, the defense was based on the premise that she was a hostage, forced by Starkweather to accompany her in her murderous madness. It was not a very credible defense, and, like Charlie, she was convicted of murder on 28 November 1958.

Because she was just fourteen at the time of the events, she was sentenced to life imprisonment instead of the electric chair. She served her sentence at the Nebraska Center for Women until her parole in June 1976, after 18 years in prison.

In 2007, she married Fredrick Clair, a meteorologist from Michigan. Five years later, she was the victim of a bad car accident in which her husband lost his life.

In 2023, Caril Fugate was the subject of a Showtime documentary entitled *The Twelfth Victim*. She is presented as a teenage victim of Starkweather's grip, too young and too fragile to have committed any

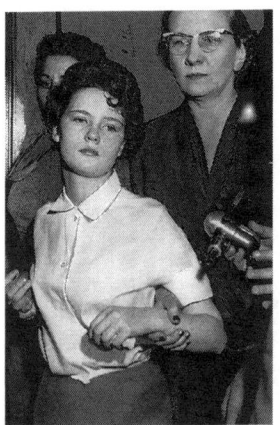

The natural born killers ended up in shackles.

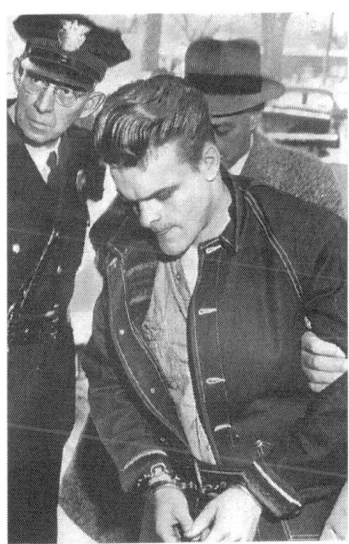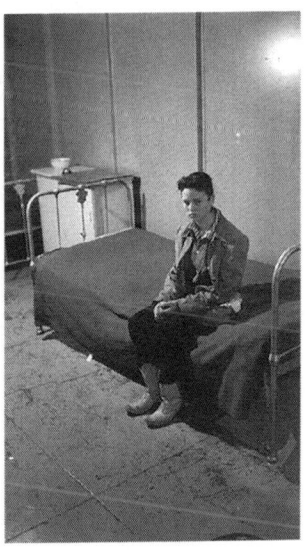

crime, contrary to what had been said by the media at the time of the murders. Did her youth excuse her passivity? Was she just another hostage, the victim of a real psychopath? Or, on the contrary, was she the muse of Charlie Starkweather, a small-time criminal who became a crime celebrity who, during those few weeks, had gone trigger-happy to impress his beauty?

Gerald and Charlene Gallego

California, in the '70s and '80s, was a popular territory for serial killers. The Gallegos, a couple from Sacramento, are not on the list of the most famous serial killers, but they still kidnapped and killed ten people, which is nothing to sniff at. Most of their victims were teenage girls, captured for the purpose of obtaining a regular supply of "disposable sex slaves." According to the versions available in the press, Charlene Gallego was either a reluctant follower or a consenting participant in her husband's murder spree. After the couple was apprehended, Charlene claimed that Gerald beat her and intimidated her into helping him kill, but Gerald on the other hand, insisted that she had been involved in the attacks and murders. "We shared the same sexual fantasy, and we just made it happen," Charlene later said. "I mean, it was easy and fun, and we had a good time, so why not do it?"

Gerald Armond Gallego was the very embodiment of a criminal with heavy heredity. He was born on 17

July 1946, when his father, whom he would never meet, was imprisoned in San Quentin for the murder of two policemen. In fact, in 1955, Gerald Albert Gallego received the dubious distinction of being the first man to be executed in the new gas chamber of Mississippi.

Gerald's mother was no stranger to delinquency, having been raised in a family that included murderers and child molesters. Lorraine Pullen Bennett Gallego was a prostitute in Sacramento, and her boy Gerald served as a lookout, and a punching-bag, for various pimps in the 1950s.

Charlene Gallego's childhood was a fairytale. She was born Charlene Williams in 1956 from Charles and Mercedes Williams. Charles Williams had risen in the food industry from a job as a grocery boy to a management position in a national grocery chain. Charlene was an only child and grew up in Arden Park, a middle-class neighborhood in Sacramento. She was talented and gifted, with an IQ of 160 and a definite talent for the violin. It was only when she started high school that she began to enjoy alcohol, drugs and sex without moderation. She graduated high school with great difficulty, failed university and survived two failed marriages, all in a rather short time. This does not excuse the choices she made afterwards. Before her, millions of girls had experienced long periods of teenage rebellion without giving in to sexual sadism.

Gerald Gallego, for his part, was waging his own war against society and its institutions. His run-ins with the police began when he was six. At ten, he robbed a neighbor. By the time he met Charlene in 1977, he had been arrested at least twenty-three times and had served several sentences at the Fred C. Nelles School for Boys, Preston School of Industry, the Deuel Vocational Institution, and the Vacaville Medical Centre, as well as various municipal prisons. He had also accumulated a fairly large collection of ex-wives, having married and divorced five times. Whatever his faults, Gallego easily attracted the opposite sex. Among these women was his future wife and partner in crime, Charlene.

Gerald and Charlene met in a bar in Sacramento in September 1977. "I thought he was very nice," Charlene said years later. Gerald, for his part, found Charlene's short stature and blonde hair to be to his liking. Within a few days he sent her a dozen roses with a card that said, "To a very sweet girl." They settled down together after a few weeks, and Gerald immediately made it clear to him that he was the "boss." Charlene was supposed to give him her cash income at a supermarket. He told her what clothes to wear and made no secret of his misadventures with other women. Yet, Charlene found him fascinating, much more mesmerizing than her two previous husbands, and when he told her of his fantasy of having young sex slaves at hand, she thought it was exciting. They used to bring dancers and waitresses home for threesomes, but one day when Gerald caught Charlene in bed with a 16-year-old stripper, he threw the intruder out of the window and beat her to remind her who was the master.

Gerald Gallego often boasted that his libido was so strong he needed to let off steam on young girls.

Violent fantasies,
passion and firearms:
the Gallegos' deadly
cocktail.

The couple's first victim was 16-year-old Sandra Kaye Butler, who disappeared in Nevada on June 26, 1978. She was last seen at a carnival where the Gallegos had surrendered. No details about her fate have ever been given by the "sex slave killers", as the press called them during their trial.

On September 11, 1978, Gerald was ready to do it again. He woke up Charlene (who was two months pregnant and suffering from morning sickness) and told her that he had a plan she needed to help him execute. In their Dodge van, they headed to the Country Club Plaza in Sacramento, where Gerald gave Charlene a mission: She had to spot two potential sex slaves and lure them into the parking lot in the van. She hesitated at first, fearing that she might not succeed or worse, be arrested. Gerald told her that she was too hesitant. Anxious to satisfy the least needs of her companion, she redoubled her efforts and concentrated on two first candidates.

Seventeen-year-old Rhonda Scheffler and sixteen-year-old Kippi Vaught spent their afternoons shopping and having fun. When Charlene (who looked to be around her age) approached them to ask if they wanted to smoke weed with her, they didn't hesitate for a second. They followed her impatiently to the parking lot, and she put them in the van. Inside, Gerald was waiting for them with a 25-gauge pistol. The girls were surprised, stunned and easily subdued. Gerald taped them up and told Charlene to keep an eye on them while he was driving.

FOLIE À DEUX

They headed east on the I-80, towards the mountains of the Sierra Nevada. In Baxter, California, they left the highway and Gerald quickly drifted away from civilization. After finding a suitable place to park, he went out into the wild with the girls, the gun and a sleeping bag, telling Charlene to wait in the vehicle. When he came back a few hours later, he told her to take the van back to Sacramento and visit some friends so he could make up an alibi, leave the van in place and come back to pick him up in their Oldsmobile.

Charlene did as she was told, and when she returned to the woods near Baxter, Gerald put the girls in the back seat of the Oldsmobile. He sat down with them and gave instructions to Charlene, who was driving until he told her to stop. On the way, he spoke as if he was going to release the captives, but when he finally ordered Charlene to stop, he told the girls to get out, knocked them down, and shot them in the head.

Gerald and Charlene got married in Reno, and decided to leave California for a while until the double murder investigation no longer made headlines. At first, things were relatively normal. Gerald worked as a driver for a meat distributor, while Charlene worked in the office of another company. But in June, Gerald quit his job again and began to work on a new plan. He wanted to get new sex slaves, and the best place to get them, he said, was the Washoe County fair.

Brenda Judd, 14, and Sandra Colley, 13, were on their way home when Charlene spotted them. She told them that she needed help distributing advertising leaflets in the parking lot, and that it was an opportunity for them to make a few dollars. When the girls agreed, Charlene told them that she needed to get more flyers from her van and led them into her trap. The three of them got into the van, and Gerald, who had been watching and following Charlene from afar, arrived a moment later. Wielding a gun, Gerald tied up the girls and headed toward I-80. On the way to the highway, he stopped at a hardware store, returning to the van with a hammer and shovel.

Gerald drove east on I-80 for a while, then headed up the hills toward Mustang. After a while, he told Charlene to get behind the wheel, as he got in the back of the van and sexually assaulted the girls. He took his time, Charlene continuing to drive further into the hills of Nevada. Eventually, pointing out to Charlene that she was driving too fast, Gerald took the wheel again. When he stopped north of Reno, he took the girls out of the van one by one and asked Charlene to follow them.

Over the next two hours, Gerald rested and watched as Charlene forced the girls to engage in sexual acts. Colley was then dragged to a creek by Gerald. He stood behind her and hit her on the head several times with the shovel. Charlene would later remember the impact in court, describing it as "a big splash, like a flat rock hitting the mud, and the girl fell to her knees and slowly tilted her face to the ground."

After killing Judd, Gerald dug a large ditch, placed the naked bodies of the two girls there and covered

107

them with stones. Charlene cleaned the van when they returned to Reno the next morning, but Gerald decided to keep his hammer and shovel. Meanwhile, although Brenda and Sandra were reported missing, there was some confusion about two other girls who had run away. Even when the girls were found, the investigation into Brenda and Sandra's disappearance was difficult. Feeling in danger, Gerald and Charlene left Reno to return to Sacramento.

Things eventually settled down. Gerald embarked on a new adventure with another woman, but it didn't bother Charlene, who was relieved that her partner was channeling his frustrations elsewhere, because Gerald could not maintain an erection when he tried to have normal sex. But as time passed, the novelty of his new conquest faded, and Gerald sought a new source of excitement. It was time, he told Charlene, to kidnap other slaves.

On April 24, 1980, Gerald and Charlene watched groups of teenagers walking in the Tower Records parking lot in Sacramento. Seeing what looked like plain-clothes policemen in the crowd, they headed to the Sunrise mall in Citrus Heights, about 20 minutes from Sacramento. They had found their first victims in a shopping center, they reasoned, so why not try again elsewhere?

Stacy Ann Redican and Karen Twiggs, both 17, were girls that were coming from a wealthy background, but they weren't smart enough to know that the offer Charlene was making them, which was a ride in a van filled with plenty of weed, would lead them to a certain death. When Gerald pointed his 357 Magnum at them while ordering Charlene to drive, they seemed more curious than frightened, as if they were participating in some kind of candid camera show. After a while, however, the principle of reality came back to them in full effect. As Charlene headed east on I-80, Gerald got in the back of the van and raped them repeatedly. From time to time, he would stop and yell directions at Charlene, and after a while they reached Limerick Canyon near Lovelock. As he had done before, he took the girls out of the van one by one and slaughtered them with a hammer. This time, however, Charlene did not let him keep his weapon; she threw the hammer out of the van window on the way back to Sacramento.

Charlene, who had aborted the year before after being persuaded by Gerald, realized she was pregnant again. Expecting the worst, she feared Gerald's reaction, and was shocked when he seemed rather happy. The idea of giving birth after having inflicted death so many times fed his ego, and besides, becoming a father provided him with an appearance of normality. He even married Charlene, using a false identity: Stephen Robert Feil. Feeling that this new marriage was helping to blur their tracks, Gallego felt his wings grow. That's when he started taking risks.

The Gallegos, who now lived under the name Feil, were on vacation in Oregon when they spotted their next victim on June 7, 1980. Yet Linda Teresa Aguilar was not Gerald's type: she was 21 years old, had dark hair and was pregnant. But when he saw her walking

109

along the highway, he decided he had to have her. He slowed down the van and asked Linda if she needed a lift. Linda, who was busy because she was coming back from the shops, agreed to get in. Charlene already knew the routine: Gerry ordered her to drive while he committed the rape. After a while, they stopped, and Charlene went for a ride in the woods, killing time until Gerry was ready to go. When he found a place that he felt was quite isolated, he pulled Linda away from the van, hit her with a stone, and then strangled her. She was still breathing as he was burying her a few meters away from the site of her murder.

The police initially believed that Linda Aguilar, who was known to her family as having an adventurous spirit, had simply lost her way. But as the days went by, suspicions grew and when her body was found later that month, police suspected her boyfriend of the murder. Although a witness reported seeing a pregnant woman get into a pickup truck the day of Linda's disappearance, circumstantial evidence accumulated against the boyfriend, who had been accused of domestic violence in the past.

Gerald became increasingly daring and impatient. It was only a month and a half before he was ready to strike again. He and Charlene spent the day of July 16, 1980, getting drunk, then headed to the Sail Inn, a bar in Sacramento. Gerald was particularly aggressive that night, but he did not seem to pay attention to Virginia Mochel, the bartender. At the time of closing, however, he told Charlene that he was not ready to go home. They waited in the parking lot, and when Virginia left after closing the bar, Gerald forced her into the van by threatening her with his 357 magnum. But this time, instead of going out into the wild, he ordered Charlene to drive the van home. Gerald stayed in the van with his prey, sheltered by the garage, while Charlene waited inside watching television. When her husband finished raping Virginia, Gerald asked her to get in the van. She was driving as he was strangling Virginia in the back of the vehicle. They dumped the body outside Clarksburg. The next day, Gerald was celebrating his thirty-fourth birthday with undisguised joy, as if nothing had happened.

Virginia Mochel had two grandchildren and she wasn't the type to go out of town without warning, so the police took her disappearance seriously. The guests of the Sail Inn reported that two strangers, a man named Stephen and his girlfriend Charlene, had entered the bar that night. The police found Gerald at his new job as a bartender, and he admitted to them that he was at the Sail Inn that night. He knew nothing of what had happened to Virginia Mochel, however. Charlene gave similar answers and casually told the police that she and her boyfriend had gone fishing that day. When Virginia's body was found, her hands were tied with fishing line, which aroused the detectives' suspicions, but it wasn't enough to make an arrest. The case was closed due to lack of evidence.

Meanwhile, Gerald and Charlene were starting to lose their sense of caution. Gerald, who beat Charlene at the slightest argument, became even more violent. In September, Charlene moved back to live with

FOLIE À DEUX

The Gallegos kidnapped and killed 8 women and 1 man.

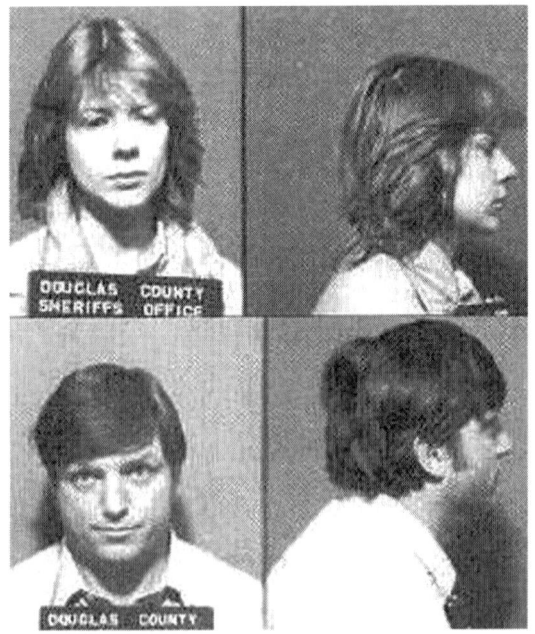

her parents. Gerald left town to take up with an old conquest. But in November, he came back, and Charlene agreed to see him again. On the night of November 1, they borrowed the Oldsmobile from Charlene's parents, telling them that they were going to have dinner out and watch a movie.

Gerald and Charlene got drunk that night, and it didn't take long for Gerald to confess to his girlfriend about his intention to kidnap other sex slaves. Both went up in the Oldsmobile, looking for new prey. Charlene was driving while he scouted out groups of teenage girls in various shopping malls for potential candidates. After a while, she realized that the game was getting more and more dangerous, and she was about to give up for the night and go home. But early on the morning of November 2, Gerald ordered her to stop the car at Arden Fair, a popular shopping mall. She was shocked to see that the next victims were not two young girls, but a man and woman, probably students.

Charlene pulled the Oldsmobile onto a parking space and Gerald got out, threatening Craig Miller and Mary Elizabeth Sowers with his gun. Hoping that obeying would prevent their drunken assailant from hurting them, they got into the vehicle. They even kept silent when a friend of Craig's, who had attended the same dinner as the couple, crossed them, leaned in the car and asked what they were doing with these strangers. Just then, Charlene, still sitting in the driver's seat, began to yell at the man and started to drive off... but not quickly enough. The young man noted down the registration number of the Oldsmobile.

Charlene drove for a while in El Dorado County until Gerald told her to stop. He ordered Craig to get out of the car and shot him in the head three times, then told Charlene to drive to their apartment. When they arrived, he took Mary Beth into the room. Charlene watched TV, and when Gerald had finished raping Mary Beth, she drove them both to the woods. He killed Mary Beth with several bullets and returned with Charlene to the apartment to get rid of the evidence.

When Gerald and Charlene returned to their parents' home the next morning, the police were waiting for them. Gerald ran away, leaving Charlene to answer the investigators' questions alone. She and her boyfriend had gone to watch a movie the day before, she told them; they were in her red Triumph. When the detectives reminded her that the Triumph was parked outside the house all night long, she told them they were so drunk that she couldn't remember which car they had taken. The detectives left with a strong suspicion.

Gerald decided that the body of Craig Miller, which he had not bothered to hide, should be moved before the police found it. But he didn't know that he had already been discovered, and when he and Charlene went looking for him that night, he was nowhere to be found. The couple decided it was time to run away. They went to Reno, where they abandoned the Oldsmobile, and boarded a bus bound for Salt Lake City.

In Sacramento, the evidence was piling up against them. Craig Miller's friend identified a photo of Gerald as the man he had seen in the Oldsmobile with Craig and Mary Beth. Charles Williams told the police that Stephen Feil's real name was Gerald Gallego. The bullets removed from Craig Miller's body matched those that Gerald shot into the ceiling of the bar where he worked.

Charlene called her parents from Salt Lake City to ask for money, and they made a wire transfer. She and Gerald made stops in Denver, then in Omaha, Nebraska, where she again called her parents. They reluctantly agreed to transfer more money, but this time they called the FBI. Federal agents were waiting for the couple at the Western Union office in Omaha, and they arrested them without resistance.

Charlene made a deal with the Sacramento DA. It took some time, but the magistrate eventually arranged for her to plead guilty to the murders of Craig Miller and Mary Beth Sowers. In exchange for her testimony against Gerald, she was given a relatively light sentence of sixteen years and eight months in prison, the minimum sentence for murder in California. She entered into a similar plea deal with the Nevada authorities, pleading guilty to the homicide of Karen Twiggs and Stacy Redican, with the same sentence as a condition. Oregon prosecutors decided to let California and Nevada bear the costs of the investigation and trial and refused to build a prosecution case. The California authorities were not satisfied with this arrangement and tried to have it cancelled, but in late 1983, a judge from the Sacramento County Superior Court dropped charges against Charlene in the deaths of Miller and Sowers. Charlene's fate was settled, the way was clear to pursue Gerald.

Gerald, still as arrogant as ever, decided to assume his own defense. But he was not very experienced in his pleadings and failed at conducting cross-examinations of the prosecution witnesses.

During the interrogation conducted by the DA, Charlene had to explain her passivity during the murders. She said that she was so afraid of Gerald that she did nothing to stop him from killing. He beat her and threatened her continuously. He kept all the money she earned, and when she expressed doubt about one subject or another, he took pleasure in demeaning her. During her cross-examination, Gerald tried to undermine her credibility by showing as evidence a love note she had written to him after their arrest. He portrayed her as an unstable drug addict and pointed out that she had a lesbian affair in prison while awaiting trial. On the last day of this tedious interrogation, Gerald finally came to the facts: "Mrs. Gallego," he said, "Isn't it the whole point of your agreement to charge me with these two murders, to save your life?" Charlene replied in a harsh tone, "No, that's not true!"

It seemed unthinkable that Gerald could do anything to further undermine his own defense, but he did. He willingly came to testify at the bar, which allowed the prosecutor to point out the countless inconsistencies in his statements. The verdict was decided quickly. On 21 June 1983, Gerald Gallego was sentenced to death for the murders of Craig Miller and Mary Beth Sowers.

After the California trial, Gerald was charged in Nevada with the murders of Stacy Redican, Karen

Twiggs, Brenda Judd and Sandra Colley. Since the bodies of Judd and Colley had not been recovered, the state's best chance of winning the lawsuit lay in the Redican/Twiggs case. Charlene showed the investigators a piece of white rope in Gerald's car. The rope matched the ligatures found on Redican and Twiggs' wrists.

Gerald's second trial began on 23 May 1984 in Pershing County, Nevada. This time he relied on a public defender, Gary Marr. Once again, his strategy was to discredit Charlene's testimony. As a star witness, she gave a detailed account of the last hours of Stacy Redican and Karen Twiggs. However, Marr was no luckier than Gerald to influence the jury, and it took them only two and a half hours to return a guilty verdict. Gerald was again sentenced to death, becoming one of the few American criminals to be eligible for death row in two separate states.

After the death sentence against him in 1984 for the murders of Stacey Redican and Karen Twiggs was overturned on appeal, Gallego was sentenced to death at a new hearing in 1999. The new jury took less than an hour to sentence him to death a second time for the murder of the two young women.

In all, Gallego was convicted of four murders. No charges were brought against him for the other six murders.

Charlene Gallego, known since the mid-1980s as Charlene Williams, was released from a Nevada

Like father, like son: Gerald's father was the first man
to be executed in the gas chamber of Mississippi.

prison in July 1997. While in prison, she had studied psychology, business and Icelandic literature. In an interview, Charlene said she was a victim too: "There are victims who have died and there are victims who have survived. It took me a long time to realize that I am one of the survivors." She also said that she "tried to save some of these girls."

She did not tell the authorities where she was going, but agreed to register as a criminal wherever she settled. Mercedes Williams, who raised Charlene's son while she was in prison, told the press that Charlene had left California and that she would never return.

On July 18, 2002, Gerald Gallego died at the age of 56 at the Nevada Prison System Medical Center. The cause of death was rectal cancer that had spread to his liver and lungs. The director of the Medical Center described him as "a very calm person. He was very reasonable about receiving no additional treatment or resuscitation efforts." Gallego made no final statement before his death.

Daniel and Manuela Ruda

To understand the crime of Manuela and Daniel Ruda, we must first understand what is "grufti" culture.

The "grufti" movement is a German subculture that shares similarities with the Gothic movement. The term "grufti" is derived from the German word "gruft," which means "crypt" or "tomb," reflecting the dark and macabre aesthetics associated with this subculture.

The grufti movement emerged in Germany in the 1980s, parallel to the rise of the Gothic movement in the UK and other western countries. Influenced by post-punk and new wave music that was popular at the time, the grufti scene was inspired by British bands like Bauhaus, Joy Division, and Siouxsie and the Banshees. The term gruftis began to be used to describe young Germans who adopted this dark and melancholic aesthetic and values. The Wave-Gotik-Treffen festival, launched in 1992 in Leipzig, becomes a major event for the world's gruftis and goths, consolidating Germany as a landmark of this scene.

Despite their morbid concerns, gruftis are hardly known for their violent outbursts. On the contrary, the image they project among their peers is that of being introverted and even extremely docile, more like the kind of people who get pushed around when they're being bullied. It is almost impossible to imagine, when you know this environment, that a grufti (or a "goth", as we call them in other countries), can pull out a knife and slice someone up. Yet it is the kind of crime that was committed by the "Satanists of Witte", a bizarre case that made the German media's headlines for a few years.

It so happens that fate has made me cross paths with one of the protagonists of this dark story, and this makes it more difficult to be impartial in the writing of this story. I shall therefore limit myself to a description of the facts, most known to the general public, as delivered during the trial, and other unpublished, told firsthand to me by this person, Manuela Ruda.

I first received a letter from Manuela Ruda in 2002, when I was living in Sweden after serving a 12-year sentence for murder. A man named Michael, who was visiting her at the time in the psychiatric ward where she was incarcerated, had shown her the cover of a book by Sondra London, *True Vampires*, which I had illustrated with a painting depicting her during her trial. She had enjoyed this painting and decided to write to me from her cell, even if she did not consider the photo that had served as my model as flattering. This was the beginning of a correspondence that lasted until the end of 2010.

But who is Manuela Ruda? Let's go back to some biographical elements.

Manuela, born Martel in 1978, was a normal child, good student and well adapted until the age of 13. Then, nobody knows why, she started to bite people at random in the street. Although she was sent to a psychiatrist for her bizarre behavior, she was not diagnosed with any serious personality disorder.

At 14, she claimed to have been visited by the devil and she began experimenting with extravagant haircuts and wearing radical "punk" clothes chosen for their shocking appearance. At 16, she dropped out of school and fled to London where she found work in a gothic nightclub in Islington, north London. She gravitated around the alternative scene of London, especially the Satanists and vampires' subcultures spiced up with black metal. She continued her experimentation with vampirism by attending "bite parties", where voluntary participants licked the blood flowing from cuts made on their arms. At 17, she traveled to Scotland where she met other goths and began to self-harm and sleep on graves. Photos of her from that time show a taciturn, overweight teenager who seemed to still be searching for her true self.

While in Scotland, Ruda wrote a letter to Tom Leppard, a local eccentric known for his leopard-spot tattoos that cover 99% of his skin.

"She was interested in me and asked if she could come visit," he later told an English newspaper. Leppard arranged for the manager of a local youth hostel to bring Ruda, then 17 years old, to his lair. She looked like an ordinary teenager, the tattooed man explains. "She reminded me of any other teenage girl. Hundreds of people have passed through here. Backpackers from Australia, Canada and Germany. I talk to a lot of them and there was nothing different about her."

The vampire continued to correspond with the leopard man on her return to Germany in 1998 and her parents even thanked him for being "her only friend". "I knew she was into piercings and playing in a heavy metal band, but things started to change and she used more radical terms," Leppard says. "Her letters became darker and full of hate."

Upon her return from England, an old friend of Manuela's described her as "eager to be the center of attention." Her behavior and look had become more extreme. She had two canine teeth removed and had fangs in their place in order to stand out from the "ignorant masses that surrounded her". She shaved her hair on each side of the head and got herself tattooed with Satanic symbols. In October 2000, Manuela claimed to have given her soul to Satan during a ceremony. Her obsession with black metal at the time led her to respond to a classified ad in *Metal Hammer*, a magazine specializing in heavy metal. That's how it all started.

The author of the classified ad was Daniel Ruda. Born in 1975, Daniel had always thought himself different and superior to those around him. He had

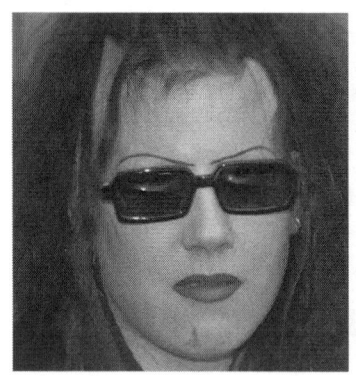 

Manuela Ruda in court.

always felt detached from his fellow men, and even as a child he often quivered at the slightest physical contact. At the age of twenty, he became active in a German neo-Nazi movement, placing posters for the National Democratic Party in the 1998 elections. His taste for the macabre and extreme led him straight to the German Gothic community where he met other extremists who practiced Satanic rituals and drank blood. Mixing Satanism and paganism in an ecumenical syncretism worthy of gypsy culture, Daniel wore pagan and anti-Christian symbols and attended concerts featuring neo-Nazi groups that encouraged the movement. However, the party's score in the election was mediocre, prompting Daniel to move away from politics and join a black metal band called the Bloodsucking Freaks. But the group struggled to provide him with the outlet he needed.

Convinced nihilist, 23-year-old Daniel ended up embracing exclusively the Satanic mystic, because it gave him the kind of life that he was looking for to channel his dark impulses. In August 2000, convinced he was a soldier chosen by Satan, he decided to place the following ad in *Metal Hammer*: "Dark-haired vampire seeks his princess of darkness who hates everything and has said goodbye to life".

Psychiatrists have commented that Daniel and Manuela would probably have distanced themselves from Satanism and vampirism if they had not met, perhaps keeping a limited interest in gothic look and music over time. Their eccentricities would probably have remained harmless, eventually fading with age.

But together, they were made for each other, and they could feed each other their darkest thoughts.

No wonder that Daniel and Manuela were immediately attracted to each other. Both were angry pariahs, and they shared a common interest in the most extreme branch of Satanism. Their idols were from the Norwegian branch of black metal, the one that had set the country on fire and blood by burning wooden churches.

The couple moved together into an apartment in Witten, where they decorated the living room with a shaped altar of plastic fake skulls. In their room there were two matching coffins in which Manuela sometimes liked to sleep. The apartment was far from warm and cozy. The windows were covered with heavy black curtains, preventing natural light from entering and contributing to the oppressive and gloomy atmosphere of the place. Behind the curtains, a sign that read "When Satan lives" warned passers-by of the beliefs shared by tenants.

The walls were painted in matte black, absorbing all light and giving a feeling of emptiness and despair. Red and black candles, scattered everywhere, provided the main source of light, creating a sinister and ritual atmosphere. The furniture was minimalist, but carefully selected to reinforce the Gothic theme. A sofa in black leather, aged and worn, faced a small table in black metal, adorned with occult engravings. Blood red velvet cushions added a touch of color.

While Daniel maintained a normal facade during the day at work, Manuela often stayed inside in her coffin, in complete darkness. Satanism had become the foundation of their relationship. Over the course of their discussions, they came to the conclusion that to truly honor the devil, it was necessary to offer him a sacrifice at his height, like the Aztec priests from the top of their pyramid.

The couple married on 6 June 2001. To complete the symbolic 6-6-6 of Satan, they decided to offer him their "offering" on the 6 of July.

Frank Hackert, 33, known as Hacki, was a colleague of Daniel's who his relatives described as warm, entertaining, popular, and a fan of the Beatles. He liked to give people the benefit of the doubt and befriended the Rudas despite their great differences. Manuela, if we refer to her statements, thought he would make a perfect jester for the court of Satan, because of his grotesque sense of humor. He would have the honor of being offered as a sacrifice. The couple's plan was to kill Hackert, drink his blood, commit suicide and walk through the gates of hell to take their rightful place alongside Satan.

On the fateful day, claiming to invite him to their home for "a farewell party", Daniel invited Hackert into their small apartment and served him plenty of drinks. The exact circumstances of the murder were later described by Manuela at her trial:

"We sat on the couch, and my husband got up. He had terrible, piercing eyes. He hit Frank with a hammer. He pulled out a knife and I said, 'Stick it right in his heart.' Frank knelt down and I saw the light go out around him. It was a sign that his soul had gone to hell. We said a prayer to Satan. We were alone in the world."

After killing their victim, they engraved a hexagram on his stomach with a razor blade and crushed numerous cigarettes on his back, while licking the blood flowing from his wounds. Both quite excited by this brutal crime, they made love in one of their coffins, while the body of their victim lay just a few meters away from them.

Not receiving any direct sign of the devil or his minions and feeling sadly human despite this considerable intake of hemoglobin intended to turn them into vampires, the couple decided it would be wise to run away. For what they thought was their last road trip, the couple headed to the cemetery where the victim of Hendrik Möbus, founder of the neo-Nazi black metal band Absurd, lay. Möbus had been convicted of the ritual Satanic murder of 15-year-old Sandro Beyer in 1998 and sentenced to 8 years in prison. Because he was under 18 at the time of the murder, he had been released, but his parole had been revoked after he gave the Hitler salute at a concert, as it was a completely illegal act in Germany. Möbus was a hero to Daniel and Manuela and going to the grave of his victim seemed like a perfect pilgrimage for their honeymoon.

At home, Manuela's mother received a farewell letter from her daughter saying: "I am not of this world" and "I must free my soul from its mortal flesh", a disturbing message that she interpreted as a suicide note. Worried about her daughter, she contacted the police who then went to the apartment and found the decaying body of Frank Hackert, with a list of 15 names considered as potential victims.

Feeling abandoned by Satan and not knowing what to do, the Rudas drove towards the cemetery until they were stopped by a patrol on July 12 near Jena, in East Germany. They surrendered voluntarily, though Daniel claimed to have no memory of the murder. In her perpetual quest for attention, Manuela could recall every detail to the police. In custody, Daniel bit his veins and asked to see a doctor, a strange behavior for a so-called vampire. He also told his lawyers that he wanted to be more famous than Charles Manson.

The trial of the Rudas began in January 2002 at the Bochum Regional Court. The case attracted considerable attention because of the macabre details of the crime and the strange behavior of the accused.

From the beginning, Manuela and Daniel Ruda claimed to be practicing Satanists, claiming that the murder was a ritual sacrifice. Daniel, a theatrical man, did the sign of the horns with his hand as soon as he arrived in the courtroom. Manuela sported a strange haircut; one side of her skull being shaved in the shape of a reversed cross. She had visible tattoos of occult symbols and a pronounced gothic look, while Daniel

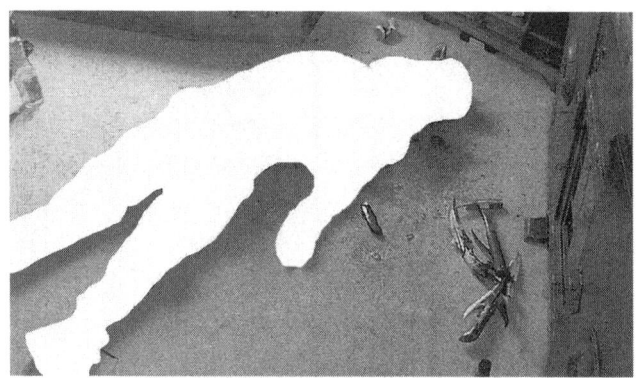

The body of Frank Hackert, censored by the German press.

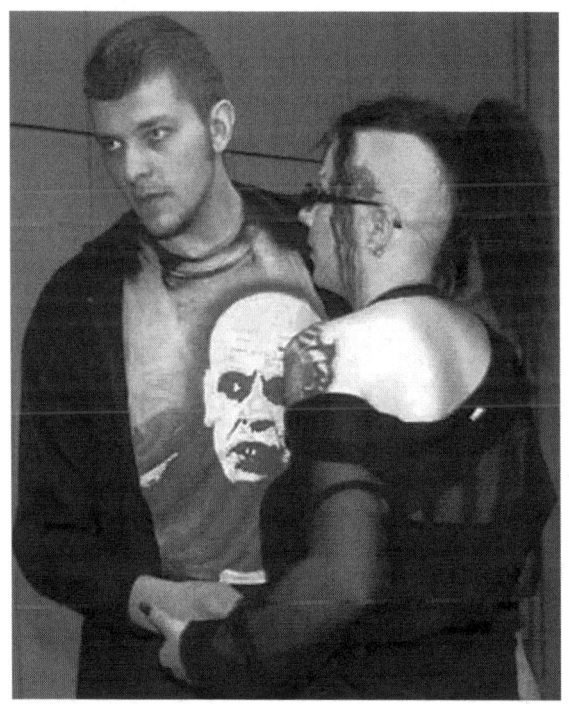

displayed a sinister smile and black clothes, reinforcing the image of a Satanic couple that the media quickly spread.

Investigators presented overwhelming evidence, including photographs of the crime scene, weapons used, and ritual objects found in the apartment. The police described the apartment as a macabre place, with walls covered in Satanic symbols and torture objects. Forensic experts testified to the brutal nature of the murder. Hackert's body had multiple stab and hammer wounds, and occult symbols were engraved on his body after death.

Manuela and Daniel Ruda gave disturbing testimonies in court. Manuela, often interrupted by chuckles or strange comments, explained that she thought she was a vampire and a Satanic priestess. She told the details of the murder coldly, explaining that Frank Hackert had been chosen as an "offering".

Daniel Ruda, for his part, supported the statements of his wife, claiming that they had acted together under the orders of Satan. He described their relationship as based on a mutual understanding of their devotion to Satanism and occultism. He insisted that the devil had pushed them to act; they obeyed only his orders, acting as instruments: "If I kill someone with my car and their bloody head lands on my bumper, it's not the car that goes to jail. The driver is guilty. I have nothing to blame myself for not doing anything." The couple showed no remorse.

Psychiatrist experts played a crucial role in the trial, seeking to determine the mental state of the accused at the time of the crime. The experts, who had examined the personal history of the Rudas, their beliefs and their behavior, described Manuela as suffering from personality disorders with narcissistic and antisocial tendencies. Psychiatrists pointed out her obsession with Satanism and vampires, which she used to give herself an identity and a reason for being. Her often unpredictable and provocative court behavior was interpreted by the audience as an obvious sign of her mental disorder.

Daniel Ruda, for his part, was diagnosed with similar disorders, but experts stressed his more passive role in the couple. He was described as being under the dominant influence of Manuela, following her directives and sharing her Satanic delusions.

When it was his turn to speak, the prosecution insisted on the premeditation and brutality of the crime. They insisted that the murder of Frank Hackert was not an impulsive act, but a carefully planned ritual. The prosecutors highlighted the evidence found in the Ruda apartment, as well as the statements of the defendants themselves.

The prosecution also stressed the danger to society posed by the Rudas, arguing that their extreme beliefs and lack of remorse made them likely to reoffend. They demanded harsh prison sentences to protect the public.

The defense, meanwhile, focused its strategy on the deleterious mental state of the accused, arguing criminal irresponsibility. The lawyers argued that Manuela and Daniel Ruda were not in full possession of their mental faculties at the time of the crime and that they were under the influence of paranoid delusions.

The defense lawyers demanded that the Rudas be placed in a psychiatric institution rather than a prison, arguing that they needed medical treatment rather than punishment.

On 31 January 2002, after several weeks of trial, the court handed down its verdict: Manuela and Daniel Ruda were convicted of murder. However, the court took into account the defense's arguments concerning the mental state of the accused. Judge Arno Kersting-Tombroke sentenced Daniel to 15 years and Manuela to 13, serving time in a psychiatric unit of the prison. The court also ordered that they should never be allowed to see each other again. In a final mocking gesture, the smiling couple shared a last passionate kiss for the cameras before being escorted to their respective cells. The judge summed up the event by saying that "this case was not about Satanism, but about a crime committed by two people with serious mental disorders. Nothing mystical happened here, just a simple murder."

The couple divorced shortly after the trial. In custody, both Rudas claimed to have strayed from the "grufti" movement. Daniel wrote a book, *Fehlercode 211*, in which he claimed to have lied when he said that Satan had ordered the murder. He claimed that he was not a Satanist, but that he was trying to protect his wife, who was the driving force behind the murder. Unfortunately for him, the book was only used to convince psychiatrists in charge of his case that he was not completely cured of his mental illness; as a result, his application for early release was denied in 2011 after serving two-thirds of his sentence. Although a new psychiatrist reported in January 2013 that Daniel was no longer a threat, he was kept in prison because of his refusal to undergo therapy.

Manuela, meanwhile, voluntarily received therapy and appeared to have repented. In 2006, she agreed to answer questions from German television. Without makeup, and showing an air of contrition, she was unrecognizable. The Witten vampire had become a distant memory.

That's where I come in.

In the spring of 2007, I was contacted by Rainer Fromm, a German journalist specializing in Satanic cults. He was obsessed with the Ruda case and had interviewed Manuela several times in prison. She mentioned our correspondence to him, which had began shortly after her conviction. With good behavior, she only had a few months left to serve. According to Rainer, Manuela wanted to meet me when she would get out of prison. Her goal? Talk to me face-to-face about how to get back to normal life. At least that is the excuse she gave to the journalist, who had vouched for her to the authorities in charge of her rehabilitation.

135

FOLIE À DEUX

Those who know a little about my background know how much the concept of "rehabilitation" goes over my head. From the correspondence I had with this Teutonic Satanic woman, it seemed clear to me that she still liked horror movies, blood and death, which only piqued my curiosity.

We were supposed to meet at a horror festival in Düsseldorf. At the last minute, I was unable to attend because of an emergency. She seemed to take umbrage, because shortly thereafter, she stopped writing altogether.

It would be twelve years before I would from Manuela again. One day, while I was browsing some messages received on Instagram, I came across a message signed with the new name that "Manuela" was using after her release from prison. This anonymous account was only showing photos of forests, lakes, etc. Remaining suspicious, I asked to give me information that only Manuela would be able to give me, which she quickly did. She had been "spying" on my account for a few weeks to see where I was in my life, before deciding to contact me again.

I was glad to hear from her. Her interests had not changed much since then, and she was happy to share with me her tribulations since she had been released from the psychiatric hospital. She was still a regular at gothic festivals and horror film conventions. She was holding down a good job with a lot of responsibilities, which had allowed her to buy a house with her companion. Her new passion was urbex, and she invited me to a new adventure: explore with her the abandoned house of Armin Meiwes, the cannibal from Rothenburg.

Once again, fate would choose otherwise. Manuela was free, but Daniel, whose existence we had never mentioned to each other, was still in prison. A few months after I reconnected with her in 2017, another trial opened for him at the Bochum court. This time, Daniel Ruda was accused of conspiracy to commission the murder of his ex-wife while she was still in custody.

According to prosecutors, he had tried to convince a woman he had met through a classified ad in 2012 to carry out this plan. Ruda, denying everything, described the accusation as being "absurd", "grotesque" and "false".

Ruda, who was working as a librarian in a prison near Dortmund, had asked the previous year to be allowed to benefit from a reduced sentence.

His lawyer Hans Reinhardt said at the time: "We want to show that he is not a dangerous man anymore. In prison, he does not take drugs or drink alcohol. His mother, who is 75 years old, visits him regularly. She only wants to see her son free before he dies, and he wants to join society, find a wife, settle down and start a family."

But Doris Hackert, the mother of his victim, had replied through a different lawyer: "I hope they won't let him out. I'm not fine. I'm mentally broken. I cry a lot. It would be a nightmare for me if they let him out."

At the trial in Bochum, the prosecution alleged that Ruda was angry with Manuela for having "dumped" him. A court spokesman said: "The plan for the woman he contacted was to get a job in the kitchen of the psychiatric unit where his ex-wife was being held, and to poison her out of revenge." But the young woman, surely realizing the sheer stupidity of this plan, went to the police instead, bringing Ruda back on the bench for inciting murder.

In the face of the charges, Ruda was adamant: "There was no murder contract. The prosecutor acted with blind zeal."

It was counting without the testimony of another prisoner, who claimed to the investigators that Daniel Ruda had told him about this Machiavellian plot. Ruda replied, "This is a blatant lie from an insignificant individual who wants to pass himself off as someone important."

His lawyer called the testimony of the so-called contract killer highly doubtful. The judge, in the absence of any other evidence, gave the ex-vampire the benefit of the doubt, and dismissed the case.

Daniel Ruda was eventually released a few months later. His victim's father commented: "He has his whole future ahead of him. All I have left is the graveyard to mourn my son."

At the end of 2017, as we were still deciding when to go on our expedition to the abandoned Meiwes manor,

Manuela sent me a panicked message: "How well do you know this guy who just left a comment on your latest post?" It referred to a complete stranger, with whom I never had the slightest interaction, who had left a meaningless comment on a meme I had posted earlier. According to Manuela, this individual looked a lot like Daniel Ruda.

Although I reassured her and told her that I did not know this guy at all, the damage was done. Our exchanges became more impersonal and distant. In early 2018, we stopped exchanging messages with each other. Her Instagram account seems to have disappeared.

Did Manuela Ruda "ghost" me, for fear of invoking the demons from her past? Or maybe she was too scared to meet the "Vampire of Paris" in real life. In any case, I understand her desire to turn her back to a life devoted to darkness. The abyss always stares back.

The Wests,
a match made in hell.

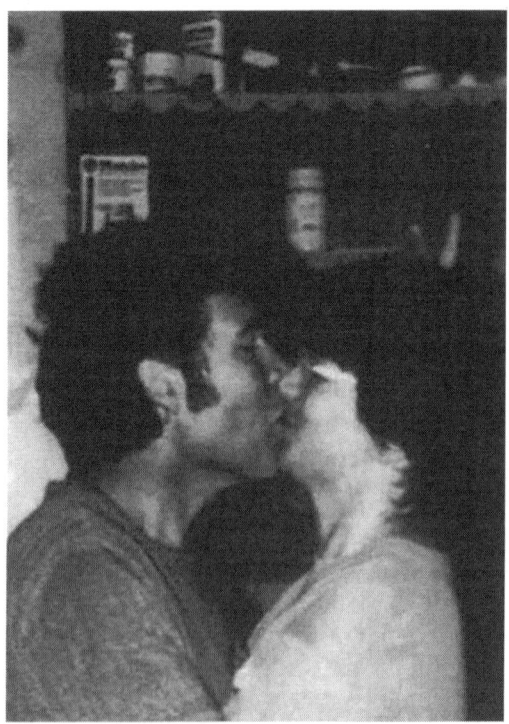

Fred and Rosemary West

Born on 29 September 1941 in Much Marcle, a small village in Herefordshire, England, Fred West was the eldest of six children of Walter Stephen West and Daisy Hannah Hill.

The West family lived in conditions of great precariousness. Their house was rudimentary, without modern amenities, and daily life was difficult. They had no electricity and the only way to heat them was a crude fireplace. Walter West, Fred's father, worked as a farm laborer, a job that was low-income and required long hours of physical labor. Fred's mother, Daisy West, supplemented the family income by also working on local farms and taking care of children. The West family lived on a rented farm, and the children were often forced to help with household chores. In addition to her six children, Daisy had two stillbirths. Fred was her favorite son.

Fred's childhood stories are tainted with violence and abuse of all kinds. According to some sources, Walter

FOLIE À DEUX

West was an authoritarian and violent man who did not hesitate to use physical force to maintain order in his home. Daisy, for her part, was a protective mother, but also abusive. It is reported that Daisy sexually abused Fred at an early age, a trauma that would have deeply affected his psychological development. Fred's older brother, named Doug, later denied the allegations.

Fred was also said to have been introduced to deviant sexual behavior at an early age. He later claimed that his father had taught him to practice zoophilia and that he also had incestuous relationships with his own children. These statements, though difficult to verify, give a glimpse of the toxic and perverse environment in which Fred evolved at a very young age.

Fred was not a good student at school. He had dyslexia, which made learning difficult. As a result, he was often the target of ridicule and harassment from his classmates. His response to this abuse was violence. Fred was known to be a brawler and undisciplined, and he quickly developed a reputation as a delinquent.

As a teenager, Fred began to show signs of criminal behavior. He was involved in several small robberies and vandalism. In 1958, at the age of 17, he had a serious motorcycle accident that left him in a coma for a week and disfigured him. This incident seems to have exacerbated his violent and antisocial tendencies. He also developed an irrational fear of hospitals. Shortly thereafter, Fred was charged with touching a 13-year-old girl, although he managed to avoid a severe conviction due to lack of evidence. A few months later, he returned to the hospital after falling two stories. A young girl, whom he had tried to touch again, had pushed him from the top of the fire escape at the Ledbury youth home, a place he frequented assiduously.

In June 1961, Fred's 13-year-old sister Kitty told her mother that Fred had been raping her since the previous December and had left her pregnant. Fred was arrested and admitted to the police that he had assaulted many young girls since his adolescence. He even asked them: "Others don't do it?" He was tried on 9 November at the tribunal of Herefordshire. Although disgusted by the actions of her son, Fred's mother was willing to testify in his defense. Immediately before her testimony at the bar, Kitty changed her mind and refused to testify, and the case was settled by a dismissal.

Fred's family largely shunned him, his mother banished him from the house, and he moved in with his aunt Violet. In mid-1962 he reconciled with his parents, but not with most of his family. He found a job in construction, which allowed him to acquire skills in masonry and carpentry. These skills would later be useful in his criminal activities, including building hidden rooms and concealing bodies.

In September 1962, at the age of 21, he met a young woman named Catherine "Rena" Bernadette Costello. Rena was a Scottish waitress who lived in Glasgow. Their relationship quickly evolved, and they married in November 1962. Rena was already pregnant with a man of Indian origin at the time of their marriage, but Fred accepted the child as his own. The couple lived with his aunt before moving to Coatbridge, where Fred worked as an ice cream salesman in a van.

In March 1963, Fred and Rena had a daughter together, named Charmaine, and later another daughter, Anne Marie, born in July 1964. However, the relationship between Fred and Rena was tumultuous, marked by violence and abuse. Fred abused his children. He kept his daughters in cages in bunk beds with bars on them. They could only get out when he went to work.

Fred later admitted to having had many affairs during the early years of his marriage and to having an illegitimate child. When Rena learned of her husband's infidelity, she began to have an affair with a man named John McLachlan. One day, Fred caught the lovers in each other's arms. He started to hit Rena. In response, McLachlan began to beat Fred, who grabbed a knife and cut the abdomen of McLachlan. He dropped his knife when McLachlan struck him with a second punch. Years later, McLachlan recalled the incident: "He could not fight as a man, but he did not hesitate to attack women."

Despite this incident, Fred and Rena continued to live together, and McLachlan could only see that his lover was increasingly covered with bruises and black eyes. Fred even attacked his children, whom he hit when they asked for ice cream.

On 4 November 1965, Fred accidentally hit and killed a little boy in Glasgow with his van. No charges were brought against him, but he lived in fear of hostile reaction and potential reprisals from the local population, to whom he owed his livelihood - ice cream man's bread. In December he returned to Gloucester with Charmaine and Anne Marie, renting a caravan at the Timberland Caravan Park in Bishop's Cleeve. Rena joined him in February 1966, accompanied by Isa McNeill and Anne McFall, two teenage girls who served as their nannies and also settled in Fred's caravan (McNeill and McFall both came from poor backgrounds and hoped to find work in England). Shortly after moving south, Fred found a job as a truck driver at a local slaughterhouse.

Far from Scotland, Fred revealed his true face to the three women who lived under his roof. He was prone to violent mood swings, and it was Rena and McNeill who paid the price. It was at this time that he also began to sexually abuse Charmaine and encouraged Rena to turn to prostitution to supplement her meager income.

No longer able to bear the blows, Rena fled with Isa, but left her two daughters Anne Marie and Charmaine behind. Anne McFall, still a minor, remained under Fred's thumb and tried to persuade him to finalize his divorce with Rena in order to marry her.

In July 1967, Anne, who was then 8 months pregnant, disappeared overnight. Bone fragments belonging to her were found years later, in June 1994, near a corn field. Her bones had been carefully disarticulated and several phalanges were missing. There was no sign of the fetus in her abdomen. Fred would never confess to the first murder to the investigators, but he would go on to boast about it to a prison visitor after his arrest. He stabbed her after an argument, but according to the coroner's office, this did not explain the presence of ligature marks around the victim's wrists.

Fred met Rosemary Letts in early 1969, shortly after her 15th birthday. They met while waiting for the same bus at Cheltenham. At first, Rose was repulsed by the neglected appearance of Fred, then 28 years old, and deduced that he was a homeless man, but she was quickly flattered by the attention that Fred continued to give her over the next few days, while he was always sitting next to her at the same bus stop. Rose twice refused to go on a date with Fred, but she let him take her home. In their first conversations, Fred soon discovered that although Rose had never had a boyfriend, she was far from being prude. To gain his sympathy, he told her that he and his two daughters had been abandoned by their wife and that he wished to have more children.

Rose West was born Rosemary Pauline Letts in Northam, Devon, to William Andrew "Bill" Letts and Daisy Gwendoline Fuller after a difficult pregnancy. She was the fifth of seven children born to this particularly poor family. Rose's mother suffered from chronic depression and received shock therapy during and immediately after her pregnancy; some experts have stated that this treatment may have adversely affected the prenatal development of her daughter.

Rose Letts was a morose teenager, prone to daydreaming and poor academic performance. After her parents' separation, she first lived with her mother and attended Cleeve's school for six months, then moved in with her father to Bishop's Cleeve, near Cheltenham, in Gloucestershire. Rose's father, who suffered from paranoid schizophrenia, was prone to extreme violence and repeatedly sexually abused Rose and her older sister Patricia.

At the beginning of puberty, Rose, apparently fascinated by her developing body, was parading half-naked in the house in the presence of her younger brother, Graham (born 1957). On many occasions, at the age of 13, she also snuck into the bed of nine-year-old Graham at nightfall and sexually assaulted him.

After finding out that Rose worked at a nearby bakery, days after they first met, Fred persuaded a passerby to enter the shop and give the young woman a gift, while explaining that a "man outside" had asked her to give her this gift. Fred went into the bakery a few minutes later and asked Rose to go out with him that evening, and she accepted his offer. It was through this romantic subterfuge of another time that one of the most diabolical couples in criminal history was born.

Soon after, Rose began to openly date Fred, regularly going to Lake House Caravan Park to take care of Charmaine and Anne Marie, children who, according to her first impression, needed a maternal presence. On several occasions during their first trips together, Rose insisted that she and Fred take the girls on field trips to pick wildflowers.

FOLIE À DEUX

A few weeks after her first meeting with Fred, Rose left her job at the bakery to become Charmaine and Anne Marie's full-time nanny. Fred provided her with enough money to make her parents believe that she still worked at the bakery. A few months later, Rose introduced Fred to her family. Rose's mother, Daisy Letts, was not impressed by Fred's bragging and concluded, quite rightly, that he was a pathological liar; her father, Bill Letts, vehemently disapproved of this relationship, promising to call social services if Fred continued to date Rose. The couple decided to simply forbid Fred from dating their daughter.

Fred was 27, Rose was 15. It was easy for Rose's parents to convince social services to put her in a problem-girl center, especially since the rumor was that their daughter was prostituting herself in Fred's trailer. At the age of 16, she left the center, and became pregnant to Fred, whom she continued to see in secret. After an abortion, she left her parents' home and moved in with Fred to an apartment on Midland Road, in the city of Gloucester. On October 17, 1970, she gave birth to her first daughter, Heather Ann. Shortly thereafter, Fred was imprisoned for a few months for stealing tires.

While he was away, Rose acted like a bully with Fred's two beautiful daughters, Anne Marie and Charmaine, hitting them in turn for no good reason. The lack of reaction and crying on Charmaine's part made Rose even more furious, and she doubled the blows. The worst part was when Charmaine said, "It's okay, one day my real mom will come and get me."

Rose allegedly murdered Charmaine shortly before Fred's release date, on June 24, 1971. She is known to have taken Charmaine, Anne Marie and Heather to visit Fred on 15 June; it is believed that Charmaine was killed very shortly after this date. In addition to forensic dentistry confirming that Charmaine died during Fred's detention, other testimony from a West neighbor, Shirley Giles, corroborated the fact that Charmaine was dead before he was released. In her subsequent testimony at the Rose trial, Shirley stated that her two daughters had been playmates of Charmaine and Anne Marie when her family lived in the apartment above the West's, at 25 Midland Road in 1971. Shirley added that after her family left the apartment in April 1971, she brought Tracey to visit Charmaine one day in June, but Rose told her: "She's gone to live with her mother, and good riddance!"

In the same vein, Rose explained Charmaine's disappearance to those who asked her where the little girl was by saying that Fred's first wife, Rena West, had taken her eldest daughter to live with her in Bristol. She also informed the staff at Charmaine's primary school that the child had moved with her mother to London.

When Fred was released from prison on 24 June, he dispelled Anne Marie's concerns about her sister's whereabouts by claiming that her mother, Rena, had picked up Charmaine and she was back in her native Scotland. In her autobiography, *Out of the Shadows*, Anne Marie—who was white, while Charmaine was of Indian descent — remembers that when she asked why her mother had taken Charmaine back, but not her, Fred replied mercilessly: "She doesn't want you, my dear. You are the wrong color."

Charmaine's body was first hidden in the coal cellar on Midland Road until Fred was released from prison. He later buried her naked body in the courtyard near the back door of the apartment, claiming much later that he had not dismembered it. An autopsy performed decades later suggested that the body had been sectioned at the hip; this mutilation could have been caused by the construction work that Fred had carried out on the property in 1976. Several bones, including the kneecaps, fingers, wrist bones, toes and ankles bones, were missing from Charmaine's skeleton, which led to speculation that the missing parts had been kept as souvenirs.

Fred and Rose's next victim was the mother of Charmaine and Anne Marie, Rena. She went to Midland Road in late August 1971, telling relatives that she wanted to get her daughters back. She never returned from Gloucester. Her remains were found in 1994 next to a grove at Letterbox Field. Her dismembered body was placed in garbage bags, barely a mile from the West's apartment.

Fred and Rosemary were married on 29 January 1972. It is highly likely that Rose knew that Fred had killed Anne McFall, Fred knew that Rose had killed Charmaine, and that the couple committed a third murder together, that of Fred's ex-wife. A few months later, as Rose was again pregnant, the couple moved into 25 Cromwell Street, Fred eventually bought it from the town hall for the small sum of £7,000. Fred financed his mortgage by renting several of the rooms, preferably to young girls without ties.

But the finances remained shaky, and it was necessary to round off at the end of the month. Shortly after giving birth to her second child, Rose began to prostitute herself, working in a room on the floor of their residence. She was offering her services in a local magazine. Fred, who from his early youth fantasized about seeing his partners in the arms of other men, preferably better "equipped" than he was, encouraged Rose to seek clients in the West Indian community of Gloucester through these advertisements.

In addition to prostitution, Rose had casual sexual relations with men and women housed in their homes, and with people Fred had met in the course of her work; she regularly bragged that no man or woman could satisfy her completely. When she engaged in sexual relations with women, Rose gradually increased the level of brutality she subjected her partner to by suffocating her with a pillow or inserting increasingly bulky dildos into their orifices. If her partner resisted or expressed pain or fear, it only increased her excitement, which often made her say, "Is it too big for you, love?"

For many of these women, it was obvious that Rose and her husband (who regularly participated in threesomes with his wife and her lovers) took particular pleasure in inflicting pain on their partner. To satisfy their fantasies, the couple had amassed an impressive collection of bondage devices, magazines and

151

FOLIE À DEUX

Fred West was very attached to his tools, which
he called "him" or "her" rather than "it".

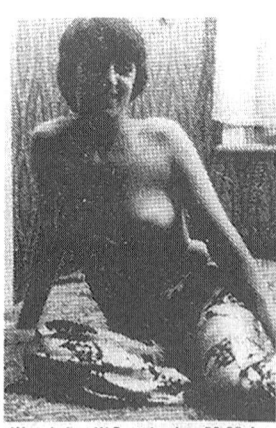

West Indian W.E. male. Age 50-60 for
sex with young housewife with view to
living in. 417673. See photo. Gloucester.

feeling in him – and a feeling   four years later she had

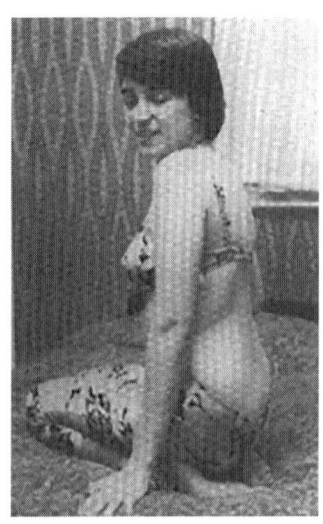

Rose West often placed classified ads
in pornographic magazines.

photographs, and then over time, he had expanded this collection to include zoophile and child pornography videos.

Fred kept two photos of his girlfriend that he had taken with him. One showed her naked in their car, impaled on the handbrake. The other showed her also naked, but this time pregnant; on her stomach was written with lipstick "My black hole", with an arrow pointing toward her pubic area.

Rose was in control of the West family's finances, with Fred giving her a salary on the weekend. The room used by Rose for prostitution was known to all in the house as "Rose's room", and it contained several holes drilled in the walls allowing Fred to watch it in action. The voyeur also had a baby monitor installed in the room, allowing him to listen to what was happening there, wherever he was in the house.

Fred was skilled with his hands, and he had especially signed the decoration of his partner's bed. At the four corners of the bed, he had glued plastic animals, more precisely a bull mounting a cow. He also made a wrought iron sign with the letters "CUNT" placed subtly above the headboard.

The room had a private bar, and a red light outside the door would turn on when Rose did not wish to be disturbed. Rose wore the only key to this room around her neck, and Fred installed a separate doorbell at the front door that Rose's clients had to press whenever they visited the house. Much of the money earned through Rose's prostitution was spent on housing improvements.

One of the sordid aspects of Rose's paid activities was undoubtedly the fact that her father Bill, after reconciling with her, became one of her regular clients. It is quite possible that among the eight children she conceived in the following years, one of them was his. At least three of these children were known to have been conceived by clients.

Children in the West family were also often exploited in many ways. As soon as they reached the age of seven, they had to participate in household chores. If they refused, they were beaten by their mother and sometimes their father. Rose, however, was careful not to leave marks on their faces, so as not to alert their teachers. In total, their children were hospitalized more than 30 times, under the pretext of having suffered domestic accidents.

The rapes were also frequent. It was often Rose who held the children to the ground while Fred raped them. When Anne Marie turned thirteen, Rose forced her to become a prostitute, claiming to her clients that she was three years older. Rose always stayed in the room when Anne Marie was with one of her clients.

In October 1972, the couple of degenerates rented the services of Caroline Owens, a young au pair. They offered her a room at 25 Cromwell Street. As often with the Wests, the proposal concealed another one, and it did not take long for the couple to make heavily supported advances. The girl was frightened and ran away, but the couple, who later met her on the side of the road, offered to take her home. The girl accepted, took a punch in the face to welcome her into the vehicle, and woke up tied to a chair, back in the house on Cromwell Street.

The rapes and tortures lasted forever. Fred whipped Caroline Owens' genitals with a leather belt, while mocking the shape of her clitoris. Rose then licked the blood that flowed from her, like a lesbian vampire straight out of a film by Jean Rollin. Pretending to become their exclusive slave, the girl offered herself to vacuum, then took advantage of this to escape through the laundry window.

The Wests were arrested and charged with assault and rape, but out of shame, Owens refused to appear on trial. The couple were fined £50 and returned to their occupations. Three months later, they killed Lynda Gough, a 19-year-old girl who was dating tenants of the house.

Lynda was subjected to torture that the Wests would later use on many victims. Her face was completely surrounded by extra strong tape, and only two small pipes stuck in her nostrils allowed her to breathe. The Wests hung her up from the beams of their cellar and carefully cut her into pieces after strangling her. The next five murders were all committed in the same place, in this sinister cellar on Cromwell Street. Some of the victims were buried on site in a shallow hole. They were all between 15 and 21 years of age. With each murder, the tortures got worse.

After the murder of Juanita Mott in April 1975, Fred dug a concrete slab in the basement and converted it into a room for his older children. The murders resumed three years later, in May 1978, with the murder of 18-year-old Shirley Robinson, one of their tenants who was pregnant at the time. This time, the body was buried in the garden. The Wests told their neighbors that the girl had gone to join her parents in Germany. A year later, the body of 16-year-old Alison Chambers joined Shirley under the garden. Like all the others, she was dismembered by Fred West, who had become a master in the art of dissection.

Of all the children in the hellish couple, Heather was perhaps the one who experienced the most abuse. Fred started raping her as soon as she reached puberty, under the pretext that: "I made you, I can do what I want with you." Her schoolmates noticed that his arms and legs were covered with bruises, and when they asked her if it was true that her mother was a prostitute, the little girl was resigned to answer in the affirmative.

On June 19, 1986, Heather disappeared from home overnight. Fred and Rose explained to her brothers and sisters that the teenager had found a job as a maid in a hotel located in a seaside town, and she left in the middle of the day, without even saying goodbye. The children, accustomed to not questioning their parents' words, did not find it strange. Months and years passed. From time to time, when one of his children did something stupid, Fred would joke that he or she would end up "under the patio, like Heather."

It was not until February 1994 that the police, alerted by the many changing versions of the Wests about the disappearance of their daughter, and the existence of the famous "joke" made by Fred West, obtained a search warrant. In addition, there was a complaint of the rape of Louise, one of the younger members of the family. On 24 February, Rose, hysterical, mumbled when the investigators asked her where her eldest daughter was: "I don't know, I can't remember! That was a long time ago! Do you think I'm a computer, or what?" Fred claimed that Heather was involved in a drug deal, and that his joke about the patio was "bullshit". Nervous, they watched as the police officers brought in a team of experts to dig. Fred went to one of his sons, Stephen, and said, "You're going to have to look after your mother and sell the house. Try to negotiate your story with the journalists, to make as much money as possible." He then went to the police himself, indicating that he was ready to confess.

According to Fred, his daughter's murder was accidental, following an argument. Rose didn't know about it, and he had secretly buried her in the garden after having dissected her with a butcher knife. On his indications, the investigators found first a femur, then other fragments scattered in garbage bags. It was Heather West. But something was wrong. Some of the fragments seemed to belong to another victim. Cornered, Fred admitted that he had also killed Shirley

25, Cromwell Street, an address forever associated with horror.

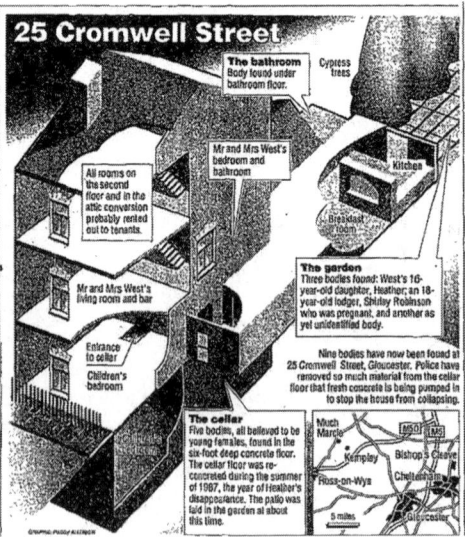

Neighbouring chapel plans prayer service for victims

Owen Bowcott

"IS there hope for our world?" asks a poster on the noticeboard outside the brick, single-storey Seventh-Day Adventist chapel.

Next door, at 25 Cromwell Street, detectives are entering the third week of their excavations in the grounds of what has been dubbed the House of Horrors. The remains of a ninth body were found under a cellar yesterday, Gloucester police announced.

The grim discoveries have not forced the closure of the church, but have added a fresh sense of purpose to the congregation's prayers.

"It brings it much closer to home when something like this happens right next door," said Pastor Ian Lorek yesterday.

He hopes to organise a special prayer service to remember those who died in the neighbouring building.

The Bishop of Gloucester, the Rt Rev David Bentley, has also announced that he wants to hold a service in Gloucester Cathedral when the search for bodies has been completed.

25 Cromwell Street

The bathroom
Body found under bathroom floor.

Cypress trees

All rooms on the second floor and in the attic conversion probably rented out to tenants.

Mr and Mrs West's bedroom and bathroom

Kitchen

Breakfast room

Mr and Mrs West's living room and bar

The garden
Three bodies found: West's 16-year-old daughter, Heather; an 18-year-old lodger, Shirley Robinson who was pregnant, and another as yet unidentified body.

Entrance to cellar

Children's bedroom

Nine bodies have now been found at 25 Cromwell Street, Gloucester. Police have removed so much material from the cellar floor that fresh concrete is being pumped in to stop the house from collapsing.

The cellar
Five bodies, all believed to be young females, found in the six-foot deep concrete floor. The cellar floor was re-concreted during the summer of 1987, the year of Heather's disappearance. The patio was laid in this garden at about this time.

Much Marcle

Kempley

Ross-on-Wye

M50 M5

Bishop's Cleeve

Cheltenham

5 miles

Gloucester

GRAPHIC: PADDY ALLEN

Robinson, a "lesbian" who had been pregnant with him and was a "friend of his".

After the discovery of these three bodies, it was decided to search the house from top to bottom. Without waiting for the result, on March 4, the serial killer of Gloucester passed a note to John Bennett, the inspector in charge of the excavations: "I, Frederick West, authorize my lawyer Howard Ogden to inform Detective Bennett that I wish to confess to nine other murders, including those of Charmaine, Rena, Lynda Gough, and others. F. West."

He said that five women were under the cellar, and a sixth was under the bathroom. Most of them were hitchhikers who met at bus stops. Fred West had a practical mind: he cut them into pieces to be arranged in cubed holes, for space saving.

Forensic examinations indicated that the victims had been subjected to unspeakable violence, tied up and had their heads taped before they died. Despite her husband's claims of her innocence, Rosemary West was arrested. She denied any involvement in the murders.

Detention was not very successful for Fred West. His visitors saw him decaying morally over the months. On 1 January 1995, the guards found him hanging in his cell. On the message he had written before committing suicide, he had drawn a tombstone with the words: "Rest in peace, Fred West. He's waiting to join his wife, Rose."

Yet Rosemary West did not seem in a hurry to join her husband in the grave. Her trial in Winchester Court began on 3 October 1995. The emphasis was on her active participation in all the murders, some links with a "feminine touch": a sash forming a loop, etc. On 22 November, Rose West was convicted of ten homicides and sentenced to life in prison.

Rose became one of the most hated women in England and spent the next few years trying to appeal this decision, but to no avail. Only Anne Marie continued to visit her in prison, with her other children cutting off all contact with her.

At Durham Women's Prison, where she was serving her sentence in the 1990s, Rose met Myra Hindley, who was then detained in the same wing. Some staff members claimed to the press that the two women were "in a relationship", a fact which was denied by both interested parties. In 2019, another British serial killer, Joanna Dennehy, told her entourage that she had been transferred to another prison after expressing her desire to kill Rose. At 70, Rosemary West continues to make a name for herself, but it seems that she will take all her other secrets to her grave.

Doug Clark and Carol Bundy

Carol Mary Bundy was born Carol Mary Peters on 26 August 1942, the daughter of Charles and Gladys Peters. Carol had an idyllic vision of her parents and childhood, and when it came to appraising her for her trial years later, it took the psychiatrists many hours of conversation to read between the lines. She could only remember the happy moments when her parents had behaved decently towards her. She described memories of her parents' celebrations at Christmas time and their efforts to make it a special moment for their three children, despite their poverty. She also remembered a time when her father claimed that the tooth fairy had visited her room while she was sleeping, making footprints with the mud-covered feet of a doll.

The memories that Carol delivered of her mother depicted her as a beautiful charismatic woman. According to Carol, one day her mother suddenly complained that she was not feeling well and told her to call her father home from work. He took Gladys to the hospital and came back several hours later alone. As soon as he walked through the door, he told Carol that her mother was dead. Carol remembered screaming. Her father held her tightly as they wept together.

It would take some time before the reality of Carol's childhood would be discovered. The truth depicts a less romanticized picture. Her father was a notorious alcoholic who dragged his family from town to town, forced to travel continuously to help out at movie theaters. Her mother was a hairdresser.

Carol was an unattractive and clumsy child, unable to meet her mother's expectations. At the age of eight, for some reason unknown to Carol, Gladys tried to get rid of her. Carol came home from school one day and found herself locked out of the house. Despite her tears and pleading, Gladys told her to leave because she was not her little girl. Only her father managed to change Gladys's mind. Carol was allowed to come home, but from that day on, Carol's mother treated her as if she didn't exist.

Charles would not allow Gladys to hit the children, but she was an angry woman, whipping them with a belt relentlessly as soon as he turned his back. Carol's younger sister, Vicky, remembered an incident. According to Vicky, Gladys had severely beaten Carol with a belt because she was sitting on a chair reading a comic book. Strangely, the little girl had quickly forgiven her mother, as if by defense mechanism; she understood that forgiving her aggressor allowed her to take control of her position as a victim.

The night of her mother's death, her father, instead of comforting Carol as she preferred to remember, had told his young daughters that they should take their mother's place in her bed. That night, at the age of eleven, Vicky was forced to give him her first fellatio. Later on, it was Carol's turn. Despite her tears and protests, her father sexually abused her daughter on several occasions. According to Vicky, their father's sexual abuse continued until he remarried eight months later. Carol remembered the first and last time as being the only events. She would always remember her father as a good man who had loved her and could not find anything wrong with this man who, yet, he had beaten and raped her many times.

Shortly after her father started raping her, Carol began running naked through the streets in the middle of the night. At the age of fifteen, Carol understood that she could get the attention she needed, even for a moment, by using her charms, especially her big breasts.

After his remarriage, Charles began to beat Carol more regularly, constantly humiliating her and telling her that she was fat and stupid. Within a few months of the wedding, Carol returned to an empty house. The cat was dead, and her father's gun lay on the living room floor. When her father returned, he told Carol that he had wanted to kill the whole family, starting with his wife, but she had taken the gun from him. Carol and Vicky were placed in foster care, then to their grandmother's home in Michigan. Within a year, their father had brought them back to California.

FOLIE À DEUX

At seventeen, to escape her father, Carol married a fifty-six-year-old man, Leonard, but she quickly left him because he was a drunkard who wanted her to prostitute herself. Shortly afterwards, she met Richard Geis, a 32-year-old writer specializing in pornography and science fiction. Finding that Carol was a smart and witty woman, Geis encouraged her to pursue her writing skills. She wrote a short story that was published in a mainstream magazine. She began writing a novel but stopped after only twelve pages. She wrote an article for a science fiction magazine. She also began to draw, but despite her talent, she ended her new career.

In 1962, Carol's father committed suicide by hanging. Geis found that Carol felt responsible for her father's death due to the sexual abuse. At this time, she began to have sex with other women. Carol went through a time when she often changed partners: if a woman disappointed her, she turned to a man, and then when he hurt her in turn, she went back to a woman. Over time, she grew tired of this game and returned to Geis.

They moved to Oregon, but soon Geis discovered her many infidelities, including the fact that she sometimes slept with other men for money. Although Geis acknowledged that Carol needed help, he did not urge her to consult. Instead, he paid for her to study nursing, provided she got good grades. She attended Santa Monica University, where they lived at the time. She graduated in 1968. Richard and Carol eventually divorced, but they would continue to be friends for many years.

Carol's marriage to Grant Bundy, a nurse she met at her workplace, was relatively stable until the birth of their first son, Chris. From that moment on, their relationship gradually deteriorated. Carol said he would demean her and beat her from time to time. At one point, she left Grant to have a lesbian affair, but returned to him after wasting thousands of dollars on her lover. When Carol's vision, which had never been good, deteriorated further, the tension between the two spouses became more acute. Grant became more violent as the prospect of taking care of their two boys and a blind Carol, who could no longer work, became increasingly apparent. Finally, in January 1979, Carol fled with her children to a shelter for battered women.

Two weeks later, she found an apartment in the Valerio Gardens complex in Van Nuys, a suburb of the San Fernando Valley, where she moved with her two sons aged 5 and 9.

When Jeanette and John "Jack" Murray, the managers of Valerio Gardens, first met Carol Bundy, she was thirty-six years old, almost obese, with greasy hair and thick glasses. Although Jeanette had known about her husband's infidelities since the early days of their marriage, she knew he liked long-legged blondes. She didn't have to worry about Carol Bundy: she was not his type. Jeanette was not worried about the number of times that Carol asked Jack to fix things in her apartment or the fact that her husband systematically took Carol to all her appointments at the doctor's and the social security office; after all, Carol was just a single mother with no great appeal.

FOLIE À DEUX

Jack Murray was born in Australia, and he had moved to America to become a singer. Although he had great potential, with an excellent voice and good looks, his arrogance tended to ruin every opportunity that presented itself. He and Jeanette were married in 1974, only ten days after they met. Shortly after their first birthday, their first child, Jessica, was born, followed two years later by their son Bryan.

In Carol, Jack had found a new audience for his stories. While he was fixing his wardrobe doors, he would tell Carol some wild stories about his adventures in the Australian army during the Vietnam War. Carol, alone and almost blind, was flattered that this handsome man would waste his time talking to her. During her visits, Carol told her about the mistreatment that her ex-husband had inflicted on her. Jack had a little sympathy for her, and after a few beers, that sympathy turned into a bit of a sex game. Carol Bundy quickly fell in love with this unexpected lover.

In no time, Carol's crush on Jack gave way to obsession. She followed him around the complex all day. If he was in the office, she was there too. Often, he called Carol from an empty apartment, and she walked down the alley, white cane in hand, to meet him. Within minutes, they were in bed. Sometimes when Jack took her to the doctor, they made love in the back of his van. Despite the fact that "making love" for Jack was limited to receiving a blow job from her, without anything in return, she firmly believed that he was taking care of her.

Over the months, Carol fell more and more in love with Jack, and she had never been happier. In a state of near euphoria, Carol spent many hours fantasizing about the wonderful life she and Jack would lead if they lived together. She even imagined having a child with him, an impossible reality, because she had her tubes ligated after the birth of David.

Carol was convinced that Jack loved her too. Without him, she would not have known that she was entitled to disability benefits and a maid. And it was thanks to Jack that she had asked for a second medical opinion about her eyes and learned that her vision could be restored surgically.

Jack was taking care of her, and she was convinced that they shared an intimacy that Jack and Jeanette had never known before. Carol believed him when he told her that in a few years, he was going to leave Jeanette. She understood him when he asked her to be more discreet and not to follow or call him. She was looking forward to the times when he would call her to have a treat in the back of the van. Carol was happy to lend him money from time to time after all he had done for her, and it gave her some hold on him. How could he leave her when he owed her money?

In October, Carol underwent an operation on her second eye. Being able to see again made her realize that her affair with Jack had not made her as beautiful and bright as she had felt. She was still fat and ugly. Jack, on the other hand, was handsome and charismatic. Any woman would want to have such a man.

It was at this time, when she was still receiving her regular disability benefits, that the $25,000 settlement for the sale of the house she had marketed with Richard came to her bank account. Carol felt rich and she went into a huge spending frenzy. She spent $4,000 on new furniture and appliances, and a fortune in beauty treatments and hairdressing. She also bought gifts for Jack, including a VCR and a new desk. This was not the first time that Carol had spent money uncontrollably. When she was married to Grant, she accumulated many credits, which put enormous pressure on their already strained finances.

Despite all the money she spent on him, things seemed to stagnate with Jack. He made her believe that Jeannette had cancer and that he couldn't leave her for her. She eventually found out his lies, but continued to believe that their love was possible. One night, hoping to meet him in one of her favorite bars, the Little Nashville Club, she saw him in Jeanette's arms, smiling and happy. Carol was depressed and took refuge in her drink, but everything changed when she saw a handsome blond man smiling at her on the other side of the room.

The man seemed to be a gentleman. During the evening, he made no sexual advances and treated her in a chivalrous manner. After taking her to another bar to dance, he promised to call her. Carol had never met someone as charming as Doug Clark, and she couldn't wait to see him again.

Douglas Daniel Clark was born on May 10, 1948, in Pennsylvania where his father Franklyn was stationed in the navy. He was the third son of five. In middle school, he chose to be called Doug rather than Douglas. The family moved regularly from Pennsylvania to Seattle, from Berkley to Japan. In 1958, Franklyn retired from the navy as a lieutenant-commander. In 1959, he moved with his wife, Blanche, and their four children, Frank Jr., Carol Anne, Doug and Jon Ronlyn, to Kwajalein, an atoll of the Marshall Islands, where he held a position as head of the Texas Transport Company's procurement department.

They spent two years in Kwajalein, living a pasha life in a subdivision that had been built specifically for the many American families who worked on the atoll. When they returned to America, they lived in Berkley for a short time before moving to India.

Other Americans living in the area have described the Clark family as nice and discreet. As for Doug, no one remembered any behavioral problems, even though his father used to stand up for him at all times.

Later, Walter and Doug were sent to Ecolat, an international school in Geneva attended by the children of UN diplomats, international celebrities and members of the European and Middle Eastern royalty. Unlike his brother Walt, who was popular and outgoing, Doug was considered to be grumpy and arrogant and made few friends. He struggled in his studies, because he was too lazy to finish his homework. Doug Clark

169

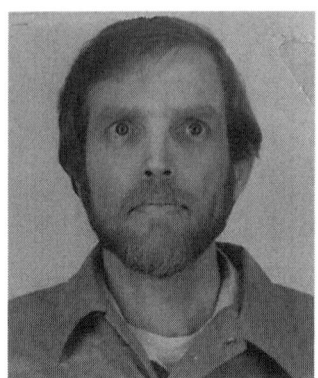

The "Sunset Strip Slayers",
an unlikely yet extremely deadly couple.

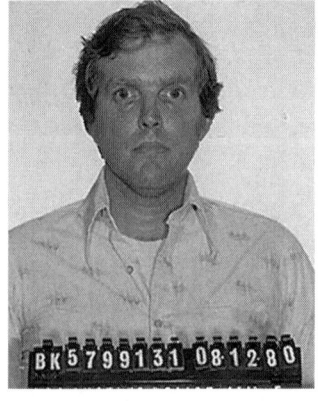

later claimed that he had developed his deviant sexual fantasies while living in Geneva.

When they returned to the U.S., Doug, 16, was sent to the Culver Military Academy in Indiana. Carol Ann had already left home by then and Walt was sent to a boarding school in Arizona; Jon Ronlyn joined him later. Doug's parents continued to move around the world, first to Venezuela and then to Perth, Western Australia.

Although intelligent, Doug was not a great student. He played a number of sports and the saxophone. In the three years he spent at the academy, Doug had no close friends, but he hung out with a group of teenagers who shared his contempt for authority. He often boasted to his friends about the wealth of his family and his sexual exploits. The fact that most of his classmates avoided him didn't seem to bother Doug.

In 1967, at the age of nineteen, just graduating from Culver, Doug went to live with his parents, who lived in Yosemite. Then he joined the air force, in radio intelligence, to make sure he wouldn't end up on the front lines in the Vietnam war. He was stationed first in Texas, then in Anchorage, Alaska, where he was responsible for decoding Russian enemy messages.

Military discipline in Anchorage reminded him of Culver and he didn't like the punishments inflicted by his senior officers, but the city's nightlife compensated for this intolerable discipline. After the army, Clark moved to Van Nuys, where he moved in with his sister Carol Ann, who lived with an abusive husband. At twenty-four, he met a 27-year-old woman named Beverly in a bar in North Hollywood and later married her. Together they bought a shop. In the 1970s, the business began to decline, and the couple was forced to sell it. To pay off his debts, Doug worked at a gas station and as a security guard.

Doug's marriage was also starting to fall apart, his wife was gaining weight and he spent most of his time in shady bars. Doug was a heavy drinker and could not handle alcohol without getting aggressive. In 1976, four years after their marriage, Doug and Beverly broke up for good.

Doug began working at the Jergens Soap Factory in 1979. His engineering duties included managing the large boiler. Although it was not a job that corresponded to his level of education, he appreciated the sense of power that came from managing this three-story structure.

In February 1980, Doug set fire to his car outside the Jergens factory while working nights to claim insurance. He later boasted to Carol that the real reason was to destroy evidence there, without specifying what kind of evidence it was.

By the time he met Carol, Doug had a knack for sneaking into the lives of unattractive women who hosted him for free, providing him with food and money in exchange for the care he gave them. When these women demanded more in return, he quickly left them and moved on to the next prey. When he was in police custody months later, he boasted to the police officers of that reputation, calling himself "king of one-night stands."

Carol remembered their first night together as incredible. Doug had been very attentive to her and seemed to really enjoy giving her pleasure. In the morning, however, she woke up to find him looking at her with a worried look. Carol insisted that he tell her what was wrong. He reluctantly admitted that he had problems with his landlady and wondered if he could come and live in her apartment. Of course, Carol agreed.

Carol's new affair had not calmed her passionate love for Jack Murray. She continued to send him love letters, in which she told him that she was ready to wait for him, because she knew that he really loved her.

Doug and Jack instantly felt hatred for each other when they first met at the Little Nashville Club. It seemed to delight Carol, who took it as a compliment. Using a well-practiced scheme, she confessed to her new lover the abuse she had suffered at the hands of her ex-lover, Jack. When she told him about the money she had given Jack and the gifts she had bought for him, Doug got angry and insisted that she stop. This indignation was feigned and only existed to establish his hold on her, but Carol seemed not to care. She didn't want to admit that her relationship with Doug was as one-sided as the one she had with Jack. He kept talking about himself and showed no interest in anything Carol had to say.

After reading an article in a magazine highlighting the importance of exchanging your most secret fantasies to have a more fulfilling sex life, Doug began to tell Carol about his desire to capture a young girl and keep her locked up as a sex slave. Together, Doug and Carol engaged in games of bondage and domination. Doug loved to test his seemingly non-existent sexual limits. Soon, fantasies began to include murder. He told her that it must feel "hot" to kill a woman, and that any woman who really loved him should be willing to kill for him. Carol was more than willing to follow him into these unspeakable fantasies. Soon enough, the fantasies of murder gave way to fantasies of necrophilia.

When Carol decided to buy a new car after getting her driver's license back, Doug chose a blue 1973 Buick station wagon for her. It was larger than any car she had ever driven, and her lack of peripheral vision made it difficult for her to maneuver, but she bought it without question. One afternoon in April, as Carol was trying to park the Buick, a knife fell from the sun visor onto her lap. Doug explained that he kept it to protect himself from potential intruders. He suggested, for the same reason, buying a gun.

On 24 April, Doug ordered two guns from a pawnshop in Van Nuys. Three weeks later, on 16 May, Carol recovered the two guns, 25-gauge Raven automatic pistols, which Carol said were toy-like because of their small size. Armed with three boxes of ammunition, she and Doug headed to Balboa Park in Encino. While Doug was sitting by the car and testing guns on a phone book, Carol stood 25 feet away to hear how loud the shots sounded. She told Doug that the detonations were no louder than the sound of a balloon being blown up and exploding.

Carol was losing the last vestiges of her self-esteem. When Doug explained to her that he no longer wanted to have sex with her because she was becoming less and less attractive, she was broken up about it, but instead of ending their relationship, she would accompany him when he picked up prostitutes and sat in the back seat while women tried, usually without success, to excite him orally.

Carol knew that Doug had done more than fantasize about a murder when he arrived home one night in late April 1980, covered in blood. There was blood on his blue denim jacket, around his mouth and on his hands. Carol took him to the bathroom and told the boys to go back to bed. The next morning, she told Chris and Spike that Doug had been in a motorcycle accident, but they saw Carol cleaning a bloody knife. Carol pretended to believe Doug's story that he had been with a girl in the car when her boyfriend attacked him. According to his version of events, Doug had used his knife on his attacker and had narrowly escaped death. The next day, Carol noticed blood stains in the Buick.

The scene repeated a week later. Doug told Carol that he had killed the boyfriend who had attacked him the previous week. Carol told the boys that someone had tried to steal the car and that Doug had fought his attacker heroically.

Still in late April, Charlene, a 22-year-old prostitute, narrowly escaped death. She was in the parking lot of a supermarket on Sunset Boulevard near Le Brea Avenue when she saw a man in a blue car stop. As she approached him to see if he wanted sex, she noticed that he was masturbating and began to walk away. He called her back and they agreed on a blowjob for forty dollars. They left together and he parked his car on De Longpre Avenue. She refused to get in the back seat with him. He told her that his name was Don or Ron; he had blonde hair, blue eyes and a mustache. As she lowered her head towards his crotch, she noticed that he had a very small penis. Before she could start, the man struck her head and put a knife to her neck.

As she struggled to escape, he stabbed her repeatedly. Miraculously, she managed to grab the blade of the knife. He said, "This is your last ride, baby," as he pressed his fingers against her neck. Barely able to catch her breath, Charlene kicked him as hard as she could and propelled herself out of the car. As she lay bleeding on the sidewalk, the man threw her jacket and shoes at her. Charlene was lucky enough to escape and later identified Doug Clark as her attacker.

On June 11, 1980, Janet and Andy Marano were looking for their daughters, Cindy and Gina. The girls had run away from home again. It had become a regular event over the past year since they had moved to Huntington Beach. It was the second marriage of

Janet and Andy and the union of their two families had been difficult. They had six children together: Janet had three daughters, and Andy had two daughters.

Cindy, 15 and Gina, 16, were doing well at their old school, where they were both popular. The school change had seen the girls' grades drop as they were spending more and more time "hanging out" in Huntington Beach. Their parents, devout Christians, had tried to maintain their parental authority with a firm hand. The girls' rebellion only worsened. They skipped school and ran away from home for days and weeks.

That night, according to Carol Bundy, on her way home from work, she came across a note from Doug telling her he had stopped by and would talk to her later. Needing the Buick for shopping, Carol went to his new girlfriend's apartment to swap her car with hers. With her own keys, she unlocked the Buick. On the back seat she found what looked like a gym bag filled with dirty clothes. When she looked inside, she found it was filled with bloody clothes, a blanket and paper towels. Forgetting her shopping, Carol took the bag with her in her Datsun and went home. On the way, she stopped at a laundromat and washed the clothes, a green dress and a little brown striped dress. The blanket was so bloody that she threw it, along with the bloody paper towels, into the trash.

Two days later, she said, Doug told her everything. He had been driving on the Sunset Strip in a Buick, on the afternoon of the 11th, when he saw Cindy and

Gina sitting at a bus stop. He stopped the car, lowered the passenger side window and tried to convince the blonde (Cindy) to ride with him. Refusing to go alone, Cindy had convinced Gina to come with her. He had parked the car in a deserted parking lot and forced Cindy to give him a blow job. He had told Gina to look away. He had grabbed the gun, which was hidden between the seat and the door, and shot Gina behind her left ear. While Cindy was sitting down, he shot her in the head. Neither of them was dead, so he shot them again: Gina in the head and Cindy in the heart.

He pushed them both onto the floor of the car and went to a rental garage in Burbank. He arrived there at about 4:00pm and parked his car across the driveway, outside the garage door. There was no one around so he covered the bodies with a blanket and dragged them inside. The bodies had bled on the floor, and he had left blood prints with his work boots. Suddenly, Gina raised her arm. Doug thought he was going to have to shoot her again, but she died shortly after. He laid the two girls on an old mattress that was on the floor. He had positioned them together head-and-tail by pushing their faces against each other's crotches, then he inserted his penis into Cindy's mouth and vagina and sodomized Gina right after.

The following Saturday evening, 14 June 1980, Carol called the Van Nuys police. She was passed on to Officer Heinlein from the Northeast Division Homicide Squad. Carol, using the name Betsy, told him that she thought her lover was responsible for the murder of both girls. She told him about the clothes she had washed, but the police said that they did not match what the girls were wearing. When she asked if either of them had been shot twice in the head, Heinlein refused to reveal details of the crimes. Heinlein and Westbrook, another officer who was listening on another phone, struggled to take this confession seriously. Before Carol could give them any further information, the call was cut off. The police assumed she had hung up.

Later that night, Doug came home and told Carol to watch the news. One of the main stories was about a man named Vic Weiss, whose body had been found in the trunk of a Rolls Royce parked in the garage of the Sheraton Universal Hotel. Doug claimed he had committed the murder earlier that day, to be accepted into a mob gang. To add even more credibility to his story, he told her that he had not placed the body in the car, and that it had been done by another member of the gang.

On Sunday, Doug suggested to Carol that they go on a ride together. Carol later told the police that he discussed with her the possibility of killing her if she betrayed him. They drove to a neighborhood near Foothill Boulevard and stopped at a ravine where, he told Carol, he had thrown away the body of a young blonde prostitute after shooting her. When the girl had seen his gun, she had yelled and kicked the gear stick, which broke. He had undressed her, kept her underwear for himself and gave the rest of her clothes to an eleven-year-old girl, who lived in the apartment across the street from Carol and who had allegedly "participated" in some of Carol and Doug's sexual escapades. When the victim's body was later found, she was identified as Marnett Comer, a 17-year-old runaway who worked as a prostitute on the Sunset Strip.

Carol and Doug both loved talking about murder. Even though Doug didn't even care about complimenting her anymore, Carol still put him on a pedestal. Thinking she was a generous and warm person who had sacrificed everything for her man, she seemed unable to understand how her attitude of total submission was only used to feed the hold of her lover on her.

On June 20, 1980, Carol joined Doug for their first murder together. At the Hughes Market on Highland Avenue in Hollywood, they noticed a blonde woman wearing cowboy boots, a little brown dress and a bolero jacket with red hearts on it. Doug waved at her. At first, she ignored him, but after a few more attempts to get her attention, she agreed to get in the car. She looked like she was seventeen and told him her name was Cathy.

Carol was sitting in the back with her 25-gauge Raven in her purse. She introduced herself as Barbara. The plan was that if Carol wanted to kill her, she would say, "Fuck, I'm having a blast." When Cathy and Doug set the price at $30, he parked behind the gas station on the corner of Franklin and Highland.

Doug couldn't get an erection under Cathy's expert fingers. He looked at Carol and shook his head to signal that he didn't want her to kill Cathy. Instead, he tried to grab his own gun, but Cathy was in the way. With his left hand, he waved to Carol to give him his gun, which she did, but she got the wrong hand. Knowing something was wrong, Cathy tried to move away. Doug shot her but she did not die instantly.

Doug told Carol to "stay cool", but Carol was not panicked. She sat quietly in the back and watched him do it with great interest.

Doug told her to get in the front seat. Cathy's head was resting on Carol's lap, bleeding on her shirt. Using the paper towels that Doug had given her, Carol began to clean up the mess. Using Doug's denim jacket to hide Cathy from other drivers, Carol struggled to undress the dying woman. Doug took Hollywood Freeway north and took the exit to Magic Mountain. Still in the darkness, they came to a dirt road along a stream. One kilometer further on the gravel road, they stopped and pulled Cathy out of the car, dragging her about twenty meters. They left her lying in the bushes without even being sure that she was dead.

Later, Doug committed another murder, alone this time. He spotted three prostitutes working together: a black girl, a petite blonde in a pink dress, and another rather plump blonde. He could not get them all into his vehicle and continued to drive. Returning later, he found the blonde in a pink dress standing alone. Her name was Exxie Wilson, she came from Little Rock, Arkansas. She agreed to go with him. They drove until Doug found a parking lot. While she started to press

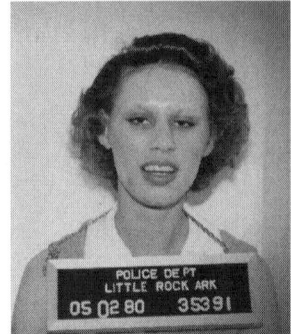

Exxie Wilson, before and after.

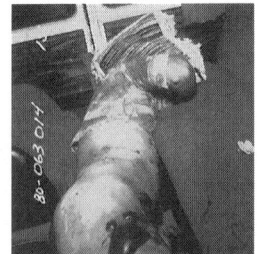

Jack Murray's body had been sodomized
with a sharp blade.

her lips against his penis, Doug shot her in the neck, and she bit him slightly by reflex. Confident that no one would see him, he dragged her out of the car, undressed her and grabbed a green ring from her right ring finger. Furious that she had been bitten him, he took a knife and cut off her head. Leaving the body in a pool of blood in the parking lot, he placed the head in a plastic bag and threw it into the back seat of the car.

Before leaving for the house, realizing that the other sex workers might be able to identify him, he returned to where he had put her in his car. The other blonde was there, waiting for her friend. She got into the car with Doug, unaware that her friend Exxie's head was behind her on the floor. Near the Burbank studios, he stopped the car and pulled out his gun. Dogs in a nearby yard began to bark. Without wasting time, he shot her in the left temple, which killed her instantly. He took off her earrings and stole her money before pushing her out of the car.

Doug Clark drove three kilometers to 240 Verdugo Avenue West, the new apartment that Carol had started renting. From there, at 3:08a.m., he called Carol, who was still living on Lemona Avenue. Three minutes earlier, a police officer found a woman in the gutter behind Burbank Studios. Her name was Karen Jones. She had left Little Rock with Exxie and turned to prostitution to feed her little boy. Concerned about the third girl, who had seen him, Doug returned to the same place where he had picked up the others. Unable to find her, he returned to Carol's apartment.

FOLIE À DEUX

Doug explained to Carol what he had done during the night. Police officers who questioned the single mother days later said she seemed to be excited at what her lover had accomplished that night. Doug had put the head in the freezer and showed it to Carol when she joined him. When she arrived, Exxie's head was lying in the kitchen sink. Doug picked it up by the hair and swung it around him in circles, bragging to Carol that he had taken her back into the shower with him and had shoved his penis inside her open mouth. They kept it in the freezer for a few more days while they were thinking about how to get rid of it.

Carol bought a nice wooden chest with brass rings and brought it back to Doug's apartment and then prepared Exxie's head. She put on nice make-up while it was still frozen. She thought she did a good job, but as usual, Doug was very critical of her and called her incompetent. Suddenly he realized that they may have left their fingerprints on the makeup. Carol had to wash it with detergent in the kitchen sink. They carefully placed the head inside the chest, which they wrapped with two plastic bags. Once the trunk was safely in the back seat of the Buick, they crossed the valley looking for an ideal place to drop it.

Eventually, they found the place they were looking for. They were about a mile west of the City Sizzler Studio, where Doug had left Exxie's body. They found an alley behind Hoffman Street, just a block from a busy artery. With the car still running, Carol took out the plastic bags and prepared to throw away the trunk. Doug hadn't completely stopped the car so she couldn't throw it very far. They heard the wood crack as they rolled over the chest with the rear tire. Doug turned to Carol, angry, calling her names, and reproaching her for not throwing it further away. He spent the rest of the night scolding Carol for her stupidity. How could she hope to become a serial killer when she was so dumb? Carol took the blame, as usual.

The head was found on the morning of 27 June. The murders on the Sunset Strip made the local sex workers much more cautious. They rarely worked alone, and it became difficult for Doug to find vulnerable prey.

Carol started to break down. She phoned her old friend Richard Geis to talk about Doug and the murders. When he told her to leave, she explained that she was unable to. A few minutes after hanging up, she called Geis again to tell him that none of this was true, she was indeed writing a story and wanted to test it just to see how real it sounded.

On August 1, Doug picked up a young prostitute. He drove to a secluded location and paid her for a blow job. He shot the girl in the neck while she was going down on him. He dumped her corpse near a water tower in the Antelope Valley, but first he laid her out on the hood of the car, while the engine was still running, and had sex with her still-warm body.

On August 3, Carol met Jack at the Little Nashville while he was drinking with an Australian woman. Carol asked him out and showed him the guns in the back of her vehicle. She told him about the murders, asking what to do. According to her version of events, he agreed to help her on the condition that she had sex with him. Carol then decided that Jack had to die because he knew too much.

Jack got into the back of the van and undressed, leaving his jeans around his ankles and his boots on. As he pushed Carol's face towards his crotch, he told her that he wanted to have sex with her 11-year-old neighbor in exchange for her silence.

These words were enough to convince Carol. She told him to lie on his stomach, drew her gun and shot him in the back of the neck. Feeling his pulse, she was surprised to find that he was still alive. She shot him again, feeling a sense of power invading her. She stabbed him in the back half a dozen times. Suddenly, she realized that it would be possible for the police to identify the bullets in Jack's head, so she extracted them with the tip of her knife. When she was done with him, she put his head in a plastic bag and took it home. On the way, she called Doug to tell him what had happened.

Together, Carol and Doug put Jack's head in a plastic bag and went to find a suitable place to throw it away. Just before sunset, Carol dumped his head in a trash can on a street near Griffith Park.

Doug was starting to panic. Carol had been seen at the bar by many witnesses, so the prospect of being caught was now very likely. He didn't want to die in the electric chair. He began to blame Carol for the situation they were in, telling her that she was stupid for killing Jack Murray without thinking of the consequences. He pointed out that the head had been cut off, but that the bullets were still in the van.

Saturday night, six days after Jack's murder, Carol and Doug headed to the Little Nashville club as usual at about 10:00 p.m. Jeanette was there, hoping that Jack would come by eventually. She had been searching for him all week in vain and suspected that he was dead. A block away, on Barbara Ann Street, a crowd began to gather around an abandoned van. Neighbors had called the police because of the foul smell. Inspector Roger Pida of the Van Nuys police went to the scene. When he opened the back doors of the van, he found Jack's body, swollen and blackened by the heat, covered in blisters. His head was not there, and he had been stabbed in the back. His buttocks were slashed and there were cuts around his anus.

The news of Jack's death soon reached the ears of the clients at the Little Nashville. The police escorted Jeanette to the station. Carol pretended to cry. Some of the bar's customers told the investigators that Jack had told them that Carol had shown him guns the week before his disappearance.

The police arrived at Carol and Doug's house the next afternoon. The couple was taken to the Van Nuys police station for questioning. Carol and Doug had already set their mutual alibis for the night of August 3, the night Jack was killed. They had agreed to tell the police that they had spent the night in bed together.

Under pressure from the investigators, Carol changed the story slightly and admitted that she had seen Jack briefly earlier in the day. She admitted to having two guns. Without further evidence, the two lovers were released.

As soon as she was alone, Carol called Richard Geis to give him all the details of the murders and her involvement and asked if she could come to see him in Portland. Geis thought she had made it up as a pretext to call him. He told her without any hesitation that he did not want her to come and that he did not wish to see her again.

Desperate, Carol decided to go out and talk to her fellow nurses. The women, terrified, immediately contacted the police. Meanwhile, Carol left the hospital, and stopped at the Jergen factory to tell Doug he was going to turn himself in. She offered him the rest of her money so he could run away, but Doug had a better plan. Behind her back, he had called the detective in charge of the investigation to tell him that Carol had gone out the night Jack was killed and that she had returned home a few hours later. Her attitude seemed suspicious, but he decided to "cover her up" without knowing what had really happened. Feigning remorse, he explained that he could no longer keep the truth quiet.

Back at the apartment, unaware of Doug's betrayal, Carol managed to reach Inspector Kilgore at the Northeast police station on the phone. She described all the murders to him and told him that she and her boyfriend wanted to surrender. At the same time, other investigators alerted by the nurses arrested Doug Clark as he was leaving the factory and went to Carol's home. She was waiting for them quietly at the door.

Once she started talking, Carol couldn't stop. The three detectives who questioned her, all very experienced, had never met a woman like her, so talkative and quick to brag about the excitement her crimes had brought her. She began by admitting that she had killed Jack because he was "a jerk who deserved to die." She said that Doug didn't force her to do anything against her will. She described the murders in detail, her involvement with Jack, Doug's sexual fantasies and their "games" with the eleven-year-old girl. She confessed that she had enjoyed killing. When the interview was over, Carol told one of the police officers that she found him sexually attractive and wondered if he was feeling the same way.

Doug, on the other hand, was extremely arrogant, but he agreed to give some evidence against her. He said he knew Cindy Chandler well, that he helped Carol get rid of Jack's head, and that he was seeing sex workers on the Sunset Strip.

During the search of the apartment, the police found a pair of handcuffs and twenty-nine bullets in a drawer next to Carol's bed, stained clothes and carpet fibers, four pairs of boots belonging to Doug, two shotguns and stacks of pornographic and bondage magazines.

FOLIE À DEUX

In Doug's file cabinet in his room, the police found a clipping from the *Valley News* about the murder of Exxie Wilson, another pair of handcuffs and a textbook with a collage of photos showing a cut penis inside the mouth of a head impaled on a stick.

In Doug's wallet, investigators found other documents that they believed linked him to some of the crimes. On a piece of paper, there was a list of phone numbers and the names of Cindy and Mindy. Mindy was the name of a girl who met Cindy the day before she died. She reported to the police that someone called her and said he was a policeman investigating Cindy's murder and he had asked her questions. The same man called again in late August to tell her he had killed Cindy, and that Mindy would be next on his list.

The "king of one-night stands" never confessed to any of the murders, telling several versions of the facts over the course of the interrogations. He insisted that Carol had framed him for murders she and Jack Murray had committed together. However, the evidence against Doug was accumulating. In his garage, investigators found a blood print that matched the exact soles of the boots Doug was wearing when he was arrested. In Carol's Datsun, they found the broken gear stick. There were three bullet holes in the rear door panel, one of which contained a 25-gauge bullet. A seat cover and a passenger side cushion were soaked in what appeared to be blood.

Two 25-caliber Raven automatic pistols were found hidden in the Jergen factory. One of the weapons was used to kill all known victims, except Jack Murray. When the Buick was found, there were bullet impacts in the driver's seat and in the backseat.

Carol's story was further verified when the remains of the woman thrown out at the water tower were found on 26 August 1980. She was given the name Jane Doe #18. The bullet found in her skull was linked to Doug Clark's Raven gun. Two days later, the mummified remains of a woman were found. She was known as Jane Doe #99. The bullet that killed her was a 25-caliber with the same characteristics as the one that killed Jane Doe #18. Cathy's remains were not found until 3 March 1981, almost seven months after the arrest of Carol and Doug. Carol was now charged with two murders. Cathy was given the name Jane Doe #28 because of lack of identification. She had been shot in the head.

In jail, Carol sent dozens of letters to Doug professing her eternal love, and she even sent a love letter to one of the members of the investigating team. Doug wrote letters to his many one-night stands, declaring his innocence and asserting the guilt of Carol and Jack Murray. He tried to maintain his influence on Carol by replying to her letters in an ambiguous manner, and even asked a cellmate to start writing to Carol so that, through him, he could continue to influence her decisions.

The psychological examinations of Carol were carried out by doctors Pollack and Cangemi. It took them five months to submit their report to Carol's defense lawyer,

FOLIE À DEUX

Sam Mayerson. They described Carol as having "a submissive personality that passes the responsibility of her actions to others." She had an average IQ, but they believed that her true potential was probably higher. They found that there was no sign of organic brain dysfunction or any indication of psychopathology. The murder of Jack Murray was probably the result of an outburst of anger and frustration at the sense of betrayal and rejection she had felt from him. In their opinion, Carol Bundy was not suffering from psychiatric disorders that had impaired her judgment.

Doug, meanwhile, used every trick in the book to delay the court proceedings. It was more than two years before Doug's trial took place in October 1982. Judge Torres presided over the proceedings. Doug wanted to represent himself, with the help of Maxwell Keith, proving the saying that "a *man* who is *his own* lawyer *has* a *fool* for a *client.*"

Although he learned a lot about the law during his two years in prison, Doug Clark was not up to the task of an experienced prosecutor. Doug repeatedly harmed his own strategy through numerous outbursts of anger and sterile arguments with the judge. Day after day, he destroyed any credibility he would have in the eyes of the jury. Not really understanding the intricacies of judicial procedures, he and his witnesses were subjected to a severe counter-interrogation and missed many opportunities to weaken the prosecution's fragile record during his own cross-examination.

Carol Bundy appeared as a witness for the defense, but Doug was no longer able to exercise the same level of control over her as in the past. Her version of events until Jack's murder had remained essentially the same for two years. Her testimony, combined with the evidence presented by the prosecution, was sufficient to destroy Doug's faltering defense strategy.

The jury began its deliberations on the morning of Friday, 21 February 1983 and rendered its guilty verdict on the morning of 28 February 1983. By the end of the first day, only two jurors were in favor of acquittal, with the majority finding him guilty. During the remaining five days, they examined all the evidence presented at the trial. They agreed that Carol Bundy was a credible, albeit somewhat pathetic, witness, one of the many women on whom Doug Clark had exerted his influence. Doug's apparent charm and obvious intelligence had initially seduced some of the jurors, but his behavior at trial allowed them to see through that facade. All of these questions, along with the ballistics evidence and Doug's lies in the courtroom, had made it clear to them that Doug was guilty.

On Tuesday, February 16, 1983, Doug Clark was sentenced to death for six murders. He was transferred to death row in San Quentin, where he made new friends with Bill Bonin, the highway killer, Larry Bittaker, the toolbox murderer, and Randy Kraft, another serial killer who enjoyed a bit of genital torture.

On 2 May 1983, the day of the trial of Carol Bundy, she pleaded guilty to two counts of first-degree murder.

In doing so, she avoided the gas chamber and was sentenced on 31 May 1990 to two consecutive sentences of 25 years to life, plus two more years for illegal use of a firearm. It was the maximum sentence possible, and her first eligible parole date was 2012, the prison system having the possibility of keeping her in prison for life if her criminal record turned out to be unfavorable after 25 years.

She was transferred to the California Institution for Women in Frontera. She continued to support Doug Clark in his struggle to prove his innocence, even though he continued to discredit her. In 1990, she handed over all her legal and psychiatric files to Doug's lawyers to help him with his defense. When asked why she still wanted to help Doug, she said that she still loved him, even though she couldn't explain why.

In the following years, Doug continued to use all available legal means to avoid execution. I started a long correspondence with him in the 90s. I remember him as a bright man, with a sense of humor that was quite dark. On one or two occasions, I remember him writing jokes about necrophilia. His hatred of Carol Bundy was as strong as ever, and through the penpals we had in common, he tried to use the resources of the then-booming internet, to share his version of the story with the public. He sometimes boasted that he had "survived" all his enemies, prosecutors, police and judges involved in his case, all of whom died from illness, accident or old age.

Among the "fans" who had written to Doug Clark was Veronica Compton, who had made the news by attempting to murder a sex worker in order to stage the innocence of another serial killer she was in love with, Kenneth Bianchi, "the Hillside Strangler." Veronica sent all sorts of naked pictures to Clark and wrote him long letters describing her deviant sexual murder fantasies.

Bundy died of a heart attack on 9 December 2003, aged 61. Doug Clark died of natural causes on October 11, 2023, at the age of 75. The basic facts of their story are sometimes evoked by uninformed YouTubers who only touch on some aspects of the perverse dynamics that characterized them. But if there is one thing to be acknowledged, it is the uniqueness of their relationship. Rarely has a couple shared such macabre fantasies, without feeling the moral constraints to satisfy them. In this, the Clark/Bundy couple was the very embodiment of the Marquis de Sade philosophy, deserving their place on the podium of the worst serial killers in Los Angeles.

Paul Bernardo and Karla Homolka

Sometimes in killer couples, the wife is the one who gets the most public reproach. There is no doubt that even though Karla Homolka has been free for a long time and owes nothing to the justice of men, her reputation as the most hated woman in Canada is not likely to be forgotten anytime soon.

Karla Homolka was born on 4 May 1970, the eldest of three sisters (Lori, born 1971 and Tammy, born 1975, murdered a week before her 16th birthday) and the daughter of Karel and Dorothy Homolka. The Homolka family, of Czech origin, settled in St. Catharines, Ontario, a few miles from Niagara Falls. After a childhood without incident, Homolka continued her schooling at the Sir Winston Churchill High School and began working in a pet store. After graduating in 1989, Homolka was employed as an assistant at a veterinary clinic in the city of Thorold (Ontario), where she was forced to resign after being suspected of stealing drugs. She subsequently found a similar job at the Martindale Veterinary Clinic.

FOLIE À DEUX

On 17 October 1987, when Homolka was only 17 years old, she met 23-year-old Paul Bernardo at the Howard Johnson Hotel in Scarborough, where she was attending a convention through her job. An hour later, they were in the same bed. The man seemed to be a heartbreaker, but against all odds, he later called Karla back on the number she had left him, and they started a more-or-less stable relationship.

Paul Bernardo was born on August 27, 1964 in Scarborough, Ontario, Canada; he was the son of Marilyn Eastman and Kenneth Bernardo. His father was known to be violent, and he was later accused by his older sister Debra of abusing her. His mother was agoraphobic and depressed, spending most of her time in their converted basement. From adolescence, Paul had always been a beautiful young blond, tall and athletic, the "ideal" man, according to many women. Nothing could make his classmates think that young Paul was a real sick man who delighted in the pain of others. One of his recurring fantasies was to build a harem of captive women. His contempt for women was aggravated at age 16, when he learnt that the man he knew as his father was not his biological father, and that he was the result of an extramarital affair. This led him to humiliate his girlfriends in public, and in private, to sodomize them, especially if the practice seemed to cause them discomfort or pain.

Bernardo was a sales manager for a multi-level marketing company specializing in wellness products. This led him to recognize a certain affinity with the main character of the book *American Psycho*, Patrick

Bateman, a multimillionaire psychopath in his spare time. Paul considered this book to be his bible, and it was found on his bedside table on the day of his arrest.

Paul was seeing Karla twice a week and seemed to give her all his attention as their relationship developed. But little by little, he began to want to control every aspect of her life. He told her what to wear, how to style her hair, what opinions to have on the fashionable subjects of society, and what to eat. He told her that she was fat and ugly. He often reproached her for not being a virgin when they had met.

What Karla didn't know yet was that her new sweetheart was wanted by the police, who only knew him by the nickname of the "Scarborough Rapist". He committed multiple, increasingly violent sexual assaults in and around Scarborough, Ontario. Most of the attacks were on young women whom he stalked after they had got off their night buses.

On 4 May 1987, Bernardo committed his first rape in Scarborough: a 21-year-old woman, outside her parents' house, after following her home. The attack lasted more than half an hour.

On 14 May 1987, Bernardo committed his second rape. He assaulted a 19-year-old woman in the garden of her parents' home. This attack lasted over an hour.

On 27 July 1987, Bernardo attempted to commit his third rape. Although he struck the young woman, he abandoned the attack after she had fought back.

FOLIE À DEUX

On 16 December 1987, Bernardo committed his third rape: a 15-year-old girl. The rape lasted about an hour. The next day, the Toronto police issued a warning to women in Scarborough who traveled alone at night, especially those taking buses.

On 23 December 1987, Bernardo committed his fourth rape. During this attack, Bernardo raped the 17-year-old girl at knife point. It was this attack that earned him the nickname of "Scarborough rapist".

On 18 April 1988, Bernardo attacked a 17-year-old girl. This fifth attack lasted 45 minutes.

On 25 May 1988, Bernardo was nearly arrested by a uniformed policeman in Toronto while spying on a bus stop. The investigator saw him hiding under a tree and chased him on foot, but Bernardo managed to escape.

On 30 May 1988, Bernardo committed his sixth rape, this time in Clarkson, about 40 kilometers southwest of Scarborough. This attack on an 18-year-old girl lasted 30 minutes.

Eight other sexual assaults took place until July 1990. As we can see, the fact of dating the beautiful Karla did not prevent Bernardo from taking great risks to pursue his career as a rapist.

On 17 November 1988, the Toronto police formed a task force exclusively to investigate the Scarborough rapist. Police did not get a meaningful lead until May 1990, when a victim provided them with a description

of the face of her assailant. The police created a sketch that was widely circulated, including in newspapers. Of the 16,000 responses received in the following weeks, three were from people who said that the portrait looked like Paul Bernardo.

Investigators interviewed Bernardo twice, while he was living with his parents in Scarborough. They were convinced he was not a suitable suspect, but as a matter of routine, they took samples from his hair, blood and saliva for DNA tests to compare with samples found on the clothes of a rape victim. DNA testing was new in Canada, and the Centre of Forensic Sciences (CFS) in Toronto had only one qualified scientist and one technician. These samples, taken from dozens of men interviewed in the Scarborough rapist case, were among the 50,000 samples collected at that time by police investigating many other cases in Ontario.

On 24 December 1989, Bernardo proposed to Homolka, a moment that Homolka considered "the most romantic of her life". In private, however, their relationship became increasingly dominating/submissive. When a close friend of Karla found a pair of handcuffs in her bedroom, she explained to him that Paul liked "role-playing". Another friend found "the list", an enumeration of things that Paul imposed on his fiancé, such as following a diet, doing sports and having impeccable hygiene. It also stated the following: "Never let anyone know that our relationship is anything but perfect; don't respond to Paul; be a perfect girlfriend for Paul; if Paul asks for a drink, bring it quickly with a smile; remember that you are stupid; remember that you are fat."

Paul became obsessed with Karla's younger sister, Tammy, 15. When Paul and Karla made love, he asked his partner to pretend to be her own sister and answer to her name as if it were hers. This unhealthy relationship culminated in September 1990, when Karla finally accepted, following his repeated requests, to help her fiancé sexually assault Tammy.

On the evening of December 23, 1990, while Homolka's parents and her younger sister Lori were sleeping, Homolka and Bernardo drugged Tammy with a mixture of alcohol/Halcion so that Bernardo could rape her. Homolka participated in the rape and filmed the sexual assault of her sister. To keep Tammy unconscious, Karla gave her halothane, an anesthetic for animals that she had obtained at the veterinary clinic.

Early on the morning of December 24, Tammy, still unconscious, regurgitated and stopped breathing, choking on her own vomit. Bernardo and Homolka dressed her and dragged her to a room. They cleaned up the crime scene, hid the video tape and called 911. An ambulance took Tammy to the St. Catharines General Hospital, where she was pronounced dead.

Three weeks after the death of Tammy, Karla and Bernardo filmed a video called *The Fireside Chat,* inside the Homolkas' residence. The video was subsequently considered evidence at the trial. It started in the basement of the house and at some point, filming continued in Tammy's room. While they were in the basement, Karla admitted to Bernardo that she had enjoyed watching Paul rape her sister. She also said in the video that she would like to leave a rose on Tammy's grave. When they were in Tammy's room, Karla dressed up as Tammy and acted like her sister. Then they lay down together on Tammy's bed.

In 2001, the magazine *Elm Street* published an article in which it is implicated that Tammy's death was not an accident, and her sister deliberately gave her a halothane overdose. The magazine described Karla as a "narcissist" who was so furious with her fiancé's attraction to her sister that she had planned to get rid of her once and for all.

Shortly after Tammy's death, the Niagara police questioned Bernardo and Homolka about a bruise on Tammy's face. They accepted Bernardo's explanation that it was a mark made by the carpet when he dragged her into the room. The mark was actually caused by the halothane, administered to Tammy via a cloth pressed against her face. The medical examiners, far from suspecting that her death was not accidental, concluded that Tammy had choked after drinking too much.

On February 1, 1991, Bernardo and Homolka moved into a bungalow in Port Dalhousie, Ontario. They married in Niagara-on-the-Lake on June 29. On the same day, boaters and fishermen from Gibson Lake south of St. Catharines discovered concrete blocks cast around arms, legs, feet and a human head. The next day, another man found a human torso floating in the water. The remains were identified as those of 14-year-old Leslie Mahaffy from Burlington, Ontario. Her parents had reported her missing on 15 June. As the police investigated Mahaffy's murder, Paul and Karla Bernardo spent their honeymoon in Hawaii.

It would be years before police knew what really happened to Leslie Mahaffy. Early on the morning of June 15, 1991, as he had made a detour through Burlington to steal license plates, Bernardo stumbled upon Leslie. Bernardo parked his car and approached her, telling her that he wanted to break into a neighbor's house. Unperturbed, she asked him if he had cigarettes. When Bernardo got her in his car, he blindfolded her, drove her to Port Dalhousie and informed Homolka that they had a new victim in their possession.

Bernardo and Homolka filmed each other torturing and sexually assaulting Mahaffy while they listened to pop music. At one point, Bernardo said, "You're doing a great job, Leslie, a really good job," adding, "The next two hours will determine what I'm going to do with you. Right now, you have a perfect score." On another part of the video tape played at Bernardo's trial, the aggression intensified. Mahaffy screamed in pain and begged Bernardo to stop. He sodomized her while her hands were tied with rope. Mahaffy later told Bernardo that her blindfold was slipping, giving her the opportunity to see her attackers.

According to Bernardo, the next day, Homolka gave her a lethal dose of Halcion; Homolka would in turn say that Bernardo had actually strangled her. The result was the same, and they put Mahaffy's body in their basement.

After a dinner with their parents, Bernardo and Homolka decided to dismember Mahaffy's body and cover every part of her remains with cement. Bernardo bought a dozen bags of cement at a hardware store the next day; he kept the receipts. After Bernardo cut the body with his grandfather's circular saw, the couple made several trips to throw the cement blocks into Gibson Lake, 18 kilometers south of Port Dalhousie. At least one of the blocks weighed 90 kg.

Police were looking for clues to the Mahaffy killer, but they were not aware of any evidence linking this crime to the Scarborough rapist. Meanwhile, the death of Tammy Homolka was not considered at all suspicious.

Almost a year later, in April 1992, the Niagara Regional Police requested assistance from the US Federal Bureau of Investigation (FBI). A group of experts in criminal profiling from the FBI drew up a psychological portrait of the murderer who, they said, was a sexual predator who would probably kill again.

On 30 April 1992, the body of a naked woman was found in a ditch along a rural road at the northern end of Burlington. Her face was disfigured, and her hair shaved, but an old wound – a missing tip from her left pinky – told investigators that this body was Kristen French, 15 years old, from St. Catharines.

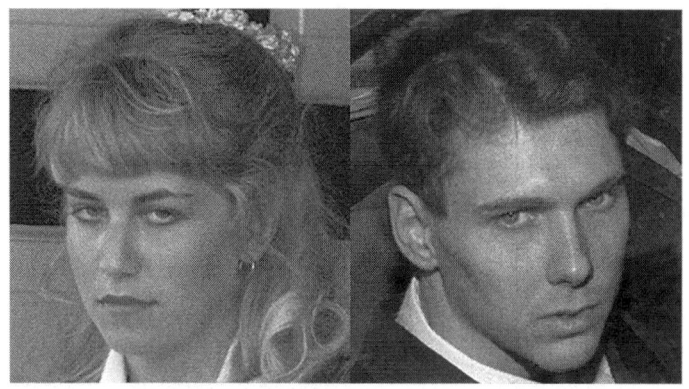

Paul often beat Karla. Did she participate in the murders
for fear of reprisal? Some experts doubt it..

 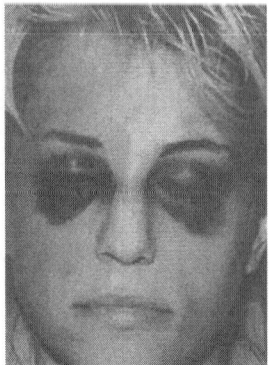

French's parents had reported her missing on April 16th. A shoe identified as hers was found in the parking lot of Grace Lutheran Church, where she passed every day to go to school and back. Then a witness reported seeing what looked like a fight in this parking lot on the afternoon of the 16th. It appeared to the witness that two people were forcing a girl into a car she described as being a cream-colored Chevrolet Camaro. Police searched the parking lot and found a torn fragment of a road map of Scarborough and a lock of brown hair. They started checking the cream-colored Camaros in the area, which turned out to be a mistake. Bernardo's car was a golden Nissan.

Police interviewed Bernardo on May 12 and again considered him not a prime suspect in what was now called the two "schoolgirl murders" in southern Ontario. Mahaffy's remains were exhumed, and the medical examiners found bruises on her back similar to the blunt wounds present on Kristen French's body. For the first time, police linked the two murders to each other. The Niagara Regional Police, in collaboration with the Halton Regional Police, established a special task force to investigate both crimes. On 21 July, a re-enactment of the abduction of French was broadcast on television. It generated thousands of calls from alleged witnesses, but no leads were substantial.

On 6 January 1993, Karla Homolka was admitted to the St. Catharines General Hospital after Bernardo had beaten her violently with a flashlight. He was arrested and charged with assault with a weapon, then released on bail. Homolka never returned to her home in Port Dalhousie.

A month later, the forensic center finally compared Bernardo's DNA to that of the Scarborough rapist. His phone was tapped.

Homolka was initially uncooperative with the police. After consulting her lawyer, she declared that she would testify against Bernardo on condition of obtaining immunity from any prosecution. The Attorney General of Ontario did not agree with this principle of immunity, but he was prepared to consider a reduced sentence. On 17 February 1993, Bernardo was arrested for the murders of Mahaffy and French, and the rapes in Scarborough.

The police put Homolka under four days of interrogation. She accused Bernardo of killing her sister. She described how her husband kidnapped Mahaffy in the yard of the girl's house, and how she and Bernardo lured French into their car parked in the parking lot. She said the two girls were used as sex slaves before Bernardo strangled them. To make matters worse, French was forced to watch television news about her father begging for her return home. Homolka said that Bernardo boasted to her about the rape of at least 30 women.

Homolka described herself as a battered woman who was forced to participate in her husband's crimes, living in permanent terror. However, a thorough search of their home led to a list of Scarborough rapes, books on deviant sexual practices, a hunting knife, handcuffs and a video showing Homolka and Bernardo having sex with two unidentified young women. Homolka was clearly a willing participant in both cases. She admitted to the police that one of the girls was drugged and later woke up not knowing that she had been raped.

On 6 July 1993, after a negotiation with the prosecutor, Homolka was convicted after pleading guilty to two counts of manslaughter for the murders of Mahaffy and French. She was sentenced to two 12-year prison terms to be served simultaneously. What the authorities did not know at the time was that the investigators who conducted the initial search of Bernardo's home had missed a series of video tapes – videos that would later be revealed to be the most damning evidence in this horrible case.

On 6 May 1993, Bernardo's lawyer recovered six 8 mm tapes that had been hidden in the Bernardo house. They were not handed over to the police until 22 September 1994. The films detailed the rape of Tammy Homolka, and the torture and rapes of Mahaffy and French. Homolka behaved like the fully consenting accomplice of Bernardo and seemed neither frightened nor coerced.

At that point, the case continued to make headlines in North America. The news of the discovery of these recordings had created public outrage. The media accused the prosecutor of making a "deal with the devil" by only giving Homolka a 12-year sentence for her role in these horrendous crimes. However, the judge was forced to respect this agreement even after these new elements had been discovered.

The selection of the jury for the Bernardo trial began on 1 May 1995. The trial lasted four months, during which Homolka spent 17 days in the witness room. Bernardo was found guilty of all charges against him: two counts of murder, kidnapping, sequestration and serious sexual assault, and a charge of barbaric acts against a corpse. He was sentenced to life in prison and was declared a dangerous offender, making his parole very unlikely.

Five years later, in 2000, the Ontario Court of Appeal and the Supreme Court of Canada dismissed Bernardo's appeal. In 2006, Bernardo's lawyer stated that his client had confessed to 10 other sexual assaults. Since 2013, he has been incarcerated at the Millhaven maximum security prison in Bath, Ontario.

Although the Bernardo/Homolka couple was officially convicted of only three murders, police suspected there were several other disappearances and rapes committed by them. Thus, it was mentioned during the trial that a 15-year-old girl, a client of the pet shop where Homolka worked, had been raped and filmed by the lovers in June 1991. The teenager unintentionally stopped the assault when she threw up. Similarly, a rape was committed in Hawaii during their honeymoon, with Bernardo keeping a press article about it at home.

The crimes of Bernardo and Homolka had a considerable impact long after the trials were over.

FOLIE À DEUX

Karla is regularly followed by the Canadian press
since she got out of prison.

The video tapes showing the rape and murder of their victims were destroyed by order of an Ontario court. Bernardo's lawyer, Ken Murray, who had recovered the VHS from their hiding place in the Bernardo house, was charged in 1997 with obstruction of justice for failing to hand over the tapes to the police. Murray was cleared of these charges in 2000.

In 1996, a government investigation into the Bernardo case revealed that the police had made many mistakes, that rivalries between different services had seriously impaired the investigation, and that some of Bernardo's crimes could have been avoided if his DNA sample had been processed and compared more quickly.

Karla Homolka served her full 12-year sentence and was released in 2005 under a series of conditions imposed by the judges, including restrictions on travel and a ban on contact with anyone under the age of 16. These conditions were overturned by another judge a few months later, which led to criticism from the Mahaffy and French families.

Homolka moved to Montreal, where she gave birth to a son in 2007. She then lived in Guadeloupe under the name of Leanne Bordelais, with her new husband, Thierry (brother of her lawyer Sylvie Bordelais), and her three children. In 2012, after being recognized in Guadeloupe by a Canadian journalist, Homolka returned to Quebec.

Paul Bernardo became eligible for parole in February 2018, after serving 25 years in prison. However, in

October 2018, his request for release was rejected by a committee of the Parole Board of Canada after only 30 minutes of deliberation. As a dangerous offender, Bernardo will probably never be released. A recent psychiatric report concluded that Bernardo "shows some degree of indifference to the impact of [his] crimes, which is consistent with information in the record that suggests that he has, over the years, always wanted to justify [his] criminal behavior in an unfounded manner".

Karla Homolka's name reappeared years later, during the trial of one of the most famous criminals in Canada: Luka Rocco Magnotta. Magnotta, who had filmed himself cannibalizing and dismembering a man he had met on the internet, had a morbid fascination for the criminal career of the "Ken and Barbie murderers". Magnotta even sent to the police one of his victim's body parts, writing as a return address the name of Karla Homolka's sister, Lori, now called Logan Valentini after a name change. Was it a tribute to her sister's crime spree? The act was intriguing, especially since Lori never had an active role in the murders. At the trial of Magnotta, in October 2014, Lori certified under oath that she had no connection with the accused. Karla Homolka, meanwhile, has never made a public statement about the actions of this embarrassing fan.

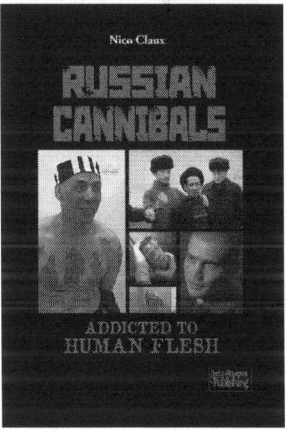

More books and products can be found on
www.serialpleasures.com

Printed in Great Britain
by Amazon

49766915R00121